"There are probably hundreds of reasons why these efforts have not been successful, but I would venture a guess that in most cases the vital importance of getting problems solved or processes improved quickly was not stressed enough....As a result, key people in the organization—busy people—ended up like monkeys stumbling around in a blizzard."

Dismayed by the number of organizations that have attempted Continuous Improvement and gained only modest results, if any at all, Charles Harwood, cofounder of the Quality Improvement Company, has consolidated his many years of experience into a simple plan that organizations of any size can use to seize the power of Continuous Improvement. The results of that effort are presented here in an engaging story about Carl, the president of Clear Run, a midsize company facing an uncertain future.

During a relentless push to reveal and identify every problem plaguing Clear Run and the people who work there, Carl and his top staff devise a plan in which everyone in the organization—from the maintenance staff to the top executive—spends an average of two hours a week solving problems and achieving opportunities.

Along the way, Carl and his team must deal with resistance, dig into some undiscussable issues, terminate and transfer a few unsupportive supervisors and managers, and change a few of their own habits and practices in order to install the effort in a rapidly growing enterprise. The results are astonishing.

Think work flow, delight your customers, improve daily and relentlessly, and do things faster are the four guiding principles that take the people of Clear Run from complacency to a fully embedded program of Continuous Improvement in less than two years. These principles and the fifteen-part change process they augment can be adopted by any organization—be it in service or manufacturing, large or small, for-profit or not-for-profit.

Kick Down the Door of Complacency

Seize the Power of Continuous Improvement

Charles C. Harwood

S^t_L

St. Lucie Press

Boca Raton   Boston   London   New York   Washington, D.C.

Library of Congress Cataloging-in-Publication Data

Catalog information may be obtained from the Library of Congress

© 1998 by CRC Press LLC
St. Lucie Press is an imprint of CRC Press LLC

No claim to original U.S. Government works
International Standard Book Number 1-57444-168-X
Printed in the United States of America 1 2 3 4 5 6 7 8 9 0
Printed on acid-free paper

To

Ma
Barbara, Carrie, Charlie, Weezie, Betty, Jane, Kit
Pete

Contents

Foreword

This is a very important book—one of the few I know of written by a former chief executive who actually practiced what he advocates both in his own organization and, after retiring, in a variety of others, large and small, for-profit and not-for-profit. Not only that, what Charles Harwood has given us here are clear, concise directions on how anyone can design, install, and operate a successful Continuous Improvement effort, and he has done it in an engaging way through the eyes of a practicing management team.

Continuous Improvement, as the name implies, is something very different from today's or yesterday's management fad. It's a process that ought to be embedded deep in the bones of any practicing management team, anywhere in the world. It's a process that, done right, involves and stimulates *every single person* in an organization. Unfortunately managers keep looking for the magic bullet that will change an organization overnight. As a result, wonderful concepts like Continuous Improvement and Total Quality Management, which work so well for the best companies, get tried then abandoned (or worse, bureaucratized) by the rest.

We have made some progress since the early 1980s, when American performance on quality was abysmal and the United States was getting thoroughly shellacked by foreign competition. But—and this is critical—we still have a long way to go. My own judgment, as a business researcher, corporate director, and entrepreneur, is that we still haven't changed enough. I regularly see operations where the Continuous Improvement process hasn't really been implemented, and it's a safe bet that all of these are kicking out mistakes at the rate of 25 to 35 percent and that the cost of fixing those mistakes (fortunately most do get fixed) is four to six times the cost of doing it right in the first place. In many hospitals your odds of getting the right drug, at the right time, in the right dose are only about 80 percent. And if you think that mistakes are just the province of notoriously bad management, look at those industries that long since ought to have it right. The hazard of checking a bag on a domestic airline springs to mind.

The interesting question, then, is: Why haven't more organizations fully embraced the Continuous Improvement ideal and had it fully implemented long ago? Most likely it's because truly adopting Continuous Improvement means that every individual in the organization must change old behaviors, and most managers I know, while great at making decisions, are awful as leaders of an implementation process. They don't recognize the difference between the control they need to exercise to make sure that an initiative stays on track and the control they must give up to allow the people closest to the action to be creative, seize initiative, and take ownership. And even if management does pass control on down the line, it usually doesn't invest in the training it takes to enable down-line employees to use that power effectively.

What this book delivers is a fifteen-part change process that gives management at all levels clear instructions on how to solve the implementation problem. By following this process anyone can turn Continuous Improvement from an interesting idea to an ingrained habit for everyone working in an organization.

The results will both help and transcend the bottom line. Leaders will feel more confident as they learn that the magic of leadership is not charisma or brilliance, which few of us have, but simply determination, patience, and enough strength of character to accept criticism, acknowledge mistakes, and keep pushing forward. With an active role in creating an environment where each person feels less frustration and receives more cooperation from colleagues at all levels, everyone in the organization will enjoy enhanced self-esteem, and morale throughout the organization will rise dramatically.

Follow the steps here, and you'll probably find that profits are up because costs are down. Follow the steps here, and you'll find that customers are happier because you are better meeting their needs for quality and service. Follow the steps here, and you'll find a lot more people enjoying work because they know that their jobs make a difference—and, because they've been involved in decisions, they are much more committed to making things work.

Happier shareholders, happier customers, and happier employees. What more can you ask?

Robert H. Waterman, Jr.
Coauthor, *In Search of Excellence*
Author, *What America Does Right*

Preface

In 1979, as president and CEO of Signetics, I introduced a management technique—now known as Continuous Improvement—to the company. The results were astounding. Over the next six years we saved $35 million due to improved operations, and our product quality improved by a factor of fifteen. Since then I have guided thirty-four other organizations through the process—organizations that varied in size from thirty-five to ten thousand employees and in function from commercial and military manufacturers to health service providers.

During this time I noticed that nearly all of the material available on Continuous Improvement was addressed to large companies and almost always implied that an outside consultant was necessary. There was precious little written for small or medium-size organizations or parts of large organizations. Yet my experience had shown that Continuous Improvement is viable for organizations of any size, with or without the additional expense of an outside consultant.

I was, and remain, dismayed by the number of organizations that have attempted Continuous Improvement and have gained very modest results or, worse, have failed completely. There are probably hundreds of reasons why these efforts have not been successful, but I would venture a guess that in most cases the vital importance of getting problems solved or processes improved quickly was not stressed enough and that managers were not adequately educated in what to do or when and how to do it. As a result, key people in the organization—busy people—ended up running around like monkeys stumbling around in a blizzard. It's no wonder that Continuous Improvement has gotten a bad rap.

I know Continuous Improvement works—it just takes the top person in the organization to lead the effort and managers willing to accept the challenge to dig inside themselves and find the courage to change, the willpower to persist, and the inspiration to lead others along a new path.

It also requires that each and every member of the organization help solve problems and seize opportunities in the work they do. To make sure it keeps working, Continuous Improvement must be institutionalized—embedded in the organization—so that as key people come and go, improvement persists. If you and those around you accept this challenge, you will be responsible for turning your organization into one that is dynamic, high-powered, and highly spoken of by its customers and clients.

In this book you will meet Carl, the president of a midsize manufacturing company called Clear Run, and journey with him as he designs, installs, and operates a major Continuous Improvement effort. At the end of two years, Carl's effort will be embedded in the ongoing management of the organization, where it will reside forever.

Clear Run is a manufacturing company, but the techniques employed are applicable to service and not-for-profit organizations as well. Consider this: only 15 percent of the people in a manufacturing company directly change a product with their own hands or tend a machine that changes a product. That means the other 85 percent are in service jobs. They are dealing with customers, making up schedules, moving things from point A to point B, doing the books, planning for the future, creating new things, purchasing materials, maintaining things, training people, writing reports—all the activities people in service organizations do.

Clear Run is a medium-size company, but the lessons can be applied to very small companies and huge conglomerates as well. Small companies might take only nine weeks to do what Clear Run will take twelve weeks to do, and conglomerates simply need to apply the process to individual sections of the company, with two thousand or fewer people and no more than five layers of management.

Once Continuous Improvement is embedded in the organization, the effort will be as unique as the organization itself. But for the first two years, as management introduces the method, every organization should do exactly the same things and learn to do them well.

Every great tennis player started out the same; he or she had to learn how to grip the racquet, hit a forehand and a backhand shot, serve and volley, lob deftly, and smash an overhead shot. Learning and practicing the basics of Continuous Improvement is what organizations need to do. Once the basics are mastered, each organization will move on to advanced methods and techniques targeted to help that particular organization.

The story about Carl and Clear Run is merely a guide, which shows how one leader applies a method composed of fifteen parts to his organization. The key to success for any organization rests in those fifteen parts, the first nine of which are introduced almost one a week from the start of the story. The last two parts appear in months 18 and 24 of Clear Run's Continuous Improvement effort. Consequently, the table of contents offers a schedule of sorts for the fifteen parts. Appendix I shows where in the story to find all the subject matter related to each part.

To ensure that individuals and organizations of all sizes and types get the most from their Continuous Improvement effort, Appendix II describes how to design, install, and operate Continuous Improvement in a variety of situations. Appendix III offers suggestions on discussion groups designed to deepen everyone's understanding. Appendix IV tells you where to go to find more information on ISO 9000, QS-9000, and the Malcolm Baldrige National Quality Award, logical next steps for the organization that has truly seized the power of Continuous Improvement.

I firmly believe Continuous Improvement is essential to the ongoing success of any organization—big or small, for-profit or not-for-profit. It should be as integral to your organization as breathing, eating, and putting on your clothes in the morning are to your life.

With this book I hope to instill that passion in you. I want you to kick down the door of complacency and seize the power of Continuous Improvement. Once you start to solve problems that have stymied you for years, to seize seemingly unobtainable opportunities, to witness the culture change taking place, and to see everyone looking forward to coming to work, you will become a believer as well.

Acknowledgments

This book could not have been written without the thoughtful input of many colleagues and friends. Therefore I offer special thanks to Gerald Pieters, Ph.D., cofounder of TQIC with me and architect of several TQM methods, and to Professor Michael Beer, Harvard Business School, for his comments on this manuscript and for a lifetime of teaching me organization development.

I also bow to the pioneers in the field of TQM such as Deming, Feigenbaum, Juran, the Japanese scholars, and P. Crosby, whose book *Quality Is Free* described a rudimentary change process.

My heartfelt thanks go to my editor Elaine de Man, and sincere thanks to many others who read my manuscript and gave helpful comments: Jeff Amacker, Oakes Ames, Bryan Down, Joe Glowacki, Greg Hampson, Skip Homan, Art Kielty, John Lowney, D.C. McKenzie, Paq McMichael, Terry Neri, David Prepelka, Andy Procassini, Joel Ramich, Glen Robertson, Ratna Sarkar, Ed Shelley, Fred Smith, and Earl Wright.

Along the way I was also most ably helped by Barbara Noble with writing advice, Mark Pearcy with assistance on the drawings, and Regina Lau and Janice Marshall with their typing skills.

About the Author

Upon graduating from Harvard and the Harvard Business School, Charles Harwood went to work for Corning, Inc., where he held a variety of jobs, including general manager of three product divisions and corporate vice president. In 1970 he was appointed CEO of Signetics, a Corning subsidiary and the sixth largest integrated circuit manufacturer in the United States. During his tenure, Signetics' sales grew from $35 million to $720 million. In 1975 N.V. Philips acquired Signetics, and Mr. Harwood remained as president and CEO until 1985. He then cofounded the Quality Improvement Company, working full time as co-general manager and consultant to clients until his retirement in 1994.

Introduction

Many organizations operate as if they are under a cloud. There may be occasional splashes of sunshine, but for the most part they have the same day-to-day problems—problems such as poor response time to customers, late deliveries, issues with quality, unreliable suppliers, and tardiness in bringing new products to market. Their costs are high because of mistakes, rework, inefficient processes, and lack of understanding between departments.

Unfortunately, many people are numb to these problems; they think it is part of their job to spend up to 25 percent of their time continually doing rework or dealing with the consequences of work—theirs or someone else's—not being done right the first time. As a result, everyone is so busy getting today's work finished that no one has time to fix the underlying causes of the problems, let alone seize opportunities that might be staring them in the face. Compounding this are bosses who give orders but don't listen and managers who place demands on people but give scant praise and little reward for a job well done. Policies, practices, and procedures are out of date. Hassles and arguments are more prevalent than wisdom and data.

The results are not good. Some people believe this is normal and just go about their business—working long, hard hours and doing nothing to improve the situation. Hopelessness reigns. A few may complain and point fingers, expressing anger and frustration. Others may simply resign themselves to the situation, shrug, and work to the minimum standard. That's no way to run an organization.

Fortunately, there is a way out. It's called Continuous Improvement—a method that involves everyone in solving operational problems and achieving operational opportunities by continuously improving work-flow processes.

Continuous Improvement was introduced in the 1920s at AT&T's telephone equipment manufacturing plant in Hawthorne, Illinois. Researchers

1

there observed that when products were made with an optimized process, there was less scrap, manufacturing time was shorter, and the products were produced more consistently to specifications. As the situation at AT&T started to improve, other manufacturing companies began to follow suit, forming quality and reliability units, writing process and product specifications, and using statistical sampling to test and observe whether products met their specifications. *Quality* became the key word, and improvement efforts were called quality control, quality improvement, or TQM (total quality management).

In the 1960s it was noted that *all* work involved processes similar to the processes in place when making a product. If improving processes could be applied to all jobs, it could, by definition, be applied to all people as well.

Once the improvement effort expanded to include everyone in an organization—not just those dealing with a product—the word *quality* and the term *TQM* did not seem as appropriate; consequently, *Continuous Improvement* began taking their place.

The most important thing to know about Continuous Improvement at this point is that in order to be successful, the effort must be led by the top person in the organization. This does not mean that the top person calls everyone into his or her office to say, "You're going to climb mountains." It means putting on the gear, pointing to the mountain in question, and taking the lead.

This is not difficult to do, but it is not a trivial task either. Continuous Improvement must be plucked out of the ongoing work to get everyone's attention and to make it a habit. The workings of the organization—including principal beliefs; the organizational vision; the day-to-day things people do; the organizational structure; the way people are measured, appreciated, and rewarded; the company's goals; what is written and talked about; the purpose and substance of the various parties; the heroes about whom stories are told; and some policies, practices, and procedures—will have to change to accept the new methodology. At the same time, any resistance to change will have to be removed. The idea is to make Continuous Improvement a permanent fixture in the organization so that it will not just dwindle away or become lost when key managers—or even the top person—change.

The second most important thing to know is that Continuous Improvement can be wildly successful with a commitment of as little as two hours a week per person—not much when you consider the staggering results that can be achieved, as you will soon see.

But first let me introduce Carl and tell you a little about his situation. Carl is the president of Clear Run, a manufacturing company in Sudbury, California, that produces electronic components for computers, telephones, television sets, and other accouterments of the modern age. It is a wholly owned subsidiary of a large, multinational conglomerate. There are 750 people at Clear Run. For all intents and purposes, Clear Run looks like a successful company, but there are problems lurking beneath the surface. It is currently growing at about 15 percent a year, but it has just come out of a bust, and that seems to be the cycle. Boom. Bust. Boom. Bust. When times are good, there is frantic hiring and expansion of facilities. Unfortunately, this is usually followed by layoffs and vacant buildings.

On top of that, everyone is putting in long hours. Many managers, supervisors, and technical people work close to fifty-five hours a week. Lunch is taken at one's desk, during a meeting, or in the cafeteria—fifteen minutes from start to finish. Morale is not very high, in spite of the boom.

Clear Run was certified to ISO 9000, albeit to a low standard of performance. Then, about a year ago, Clear Run's plant in Concord, Utah, started a TQM effort all on its own. The results on that aren't in yet. A team has recently been put together in Sudbury to improve—by a factor of one hundred—the quality and reliability of an engine-control part for an automotive customer. But these are isolated efforts, and Carl is convinced Clear Run needs something much more broad-based.

Carl is familiar with Continuous Improvement; he has read some books and articles, attended a seminar, and talked to other heads of companies—not all of whom had good things to say. Still, he wants to give it a shot. He sends a memo to each of his staff members calling for a meeting on Monday morning. Anticipating some opposition, he makes one thing clear: everyone is to attend.

The People at Clear Run

Carl, president

Carl's Direct Reports
- Carol, sales manager
- Moe, new products manager
- Nick, finance and accounting manager
- Jim, marketing manager
- Bill, operations manager
- Ferg, administration manager
- Elaine, finance and accounting manager (week 11)
- Mary Louise, Continuous Improvement counselor

Others on the Executive Continuous Improvement Team (CIT)
- Harvey, outside general business consultant
- Cam, quality manager (reports to Bill)

WEEK 1

- **A summary of the method**
- **The fifteen parts**
- **The organizational structure**

Bright and early Monday morning, the six members of Carl's staff filed into Clear Run's conference room. Carl had also invited Cam, who was not really a member of his staff but was Clear Run's quality manager, and Carl wanted him on board. He had also invited Harvey, an outside consultant with expertise in general business, human resources, and organization development.

Jim, Bill, Cam, and Ferg were full of anticipation; they had been leaning on Carl for months to do *something*. Carol looked harried, as usual, perhaps a little resentful to be called to a meeting when she had so much to do. Harvey and Nick chatted about their weekend, and Moe arrived late, talking on his cellular phone.

Once everyone settled down, Carl cut to the chase. "I am about 95 percent sure that we need to initiate a Continuous Improvement effort, and if we're going to be successful, I'm going to need the help and support of every person in this room."

Right away, he could sense a little resistance in the room, especially from Carol, the sales manager, and Moe, the manager of new products, so he decided to hit right off the bat what he knew would be their main objection.

"Now I know you're probably thinking you don't have time for this, but all I'm asking for is two hours a week. One hour for us to meet as a group and another hour to spend on specific assignments.

"To begin with, we're going to investigate the merits of Continuous Improvement—figure out where problems lurk and opportunities hide. Then, if we're all together, we'll proceed. If we're not, we won't.

"Now, assuming we do proceed, I have worked out a schedule that will carry us through the first two years.

"For the next twelve weeks we'll be learning about the method and preparing everyone in the organization to get involved. Then, from the fourth through the eighth month, our focus will be on training everyone in the organization in problem-solving techniques; we'll also start selecting problems to solve and meeting in problem-solving groups. From the ninth to the twenty-fourth month, the emphasis will be on actually solving the operational problems and achieving the operational opportunities we've identified. Ideally, by the twenty-fourth month Continuous Improvement will be purposely folded into the ongoing management of Clear Run.

"I have selected a particular method that will focus us on getting results—on solving problems and achieving opportunities, many, many of them. We're going to start and continue the effort efficiently and quickly and embed Continuous Improvement into the fabric of the organization— so that it becomes a habit, it is institutionalized, and people say, 'Continuous Improvement is something we do all the time. It is how we operate around here.'"

Cam had a question. "How are we supposed to accomplish all that in just two hours a week?"

"Let me show you," said Carl, who was obviously prepared. He stepped up to the easel at the front of the room and uncovered a hieroglyphic-looking chart (see p. 9).

"This, believe it or not, is a schematic diagram showing how most organizations are organized. In our case, that's me at the top, you guys are the next row of circles, your people are the next row of circles, and so forth. Each triangle represents one unit composed of a manager or supervisor and his or her direct reports."

He flipped the page and continued. "In order to manage Continuous Improvement, everything stays the same, but each triangle becomes a Continuous Improvement Team, or CIT (see p. 10). As a group, we are the top-level or executive CIT. Each of you is the head of a mid-level CIT. The bottom tier of triangles is the first-level CITs. These are CITs in which the members—that is, the bottom row of circles in each triangle—are not managers or supervisors.

"As the executive CIT, our job will be to *design, install,* and *operate* the Continuous Improvement effort. We will do this in weekly one-hour meetings. Then, each of you will spend thirty minutes per week meeting

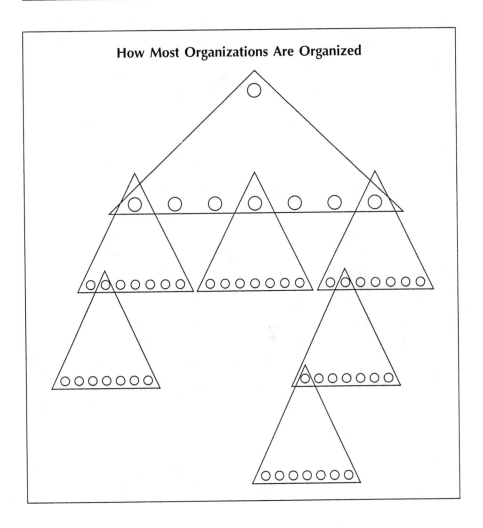

with your mid-level CITs, taking the design we establish here and *install-ing* and *operating* it throughout your area of responsibility."

Carl could see that Carol was still skeptical, so he decided to involve her directly. "Just to make sure we all understand how this is going to work with our organizational structure," he said, "I'd like Carol to bring in a chart similar to this one, detailing the organization as it falls below her. Carol, perhaps you could have that for us next week and then I'll take us through it, step by step."

By the expression on Carol's face, Carl could see she felt pressed, but knowing Carol, he knew she'd pull through. Next, Carl handed a stack of

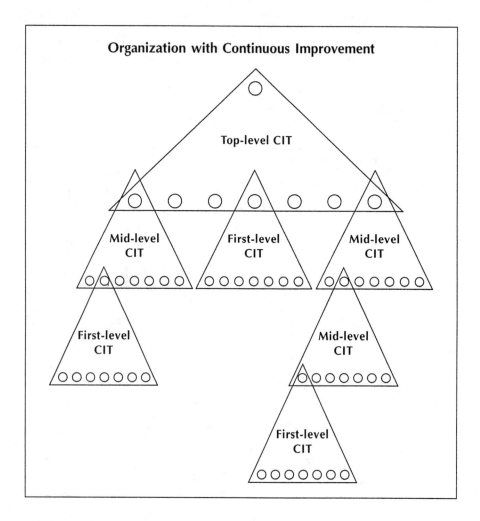

Organization with Continuous Improvement

papers to Nick, the manager of finance and accounting, to pass around the room. He then turned to the next page on the easel (see p. 11).

"These," he said, pointing to a list on the chart pad, "are the fifteen parts that make up the process—the things we have to do to design, install, and operate Continuous Improvement. This is the list Nick has just handed you.

"We will be tackling these items in sequence, one by one, in the weeks and months to come. We're already doing part 1 right now and will finish it up next week."

"Is that it?" asked Ferg, the manager of administration. "We're just supposed to follow this plan in lock step?"

The Fifteen Parts of Continuous Improvement

1. Understand the method and organizational structure.

2. Determine the need.

3. Adopt the four principles.

4. Make a four-year plan.

5. Establish vibrant communications.

6. Overcome resistance to change.

7. Form a vision.

8. Collect problems and opportunities.

9. Train everyone in problem solving.

10. Select five top-priority problems or opportunities.

11. Express the five as goals.

12. Hold everyone accountable.

13. Appreciate and reward achievement.

14. Modify prior operating guidelines.

15. Transition Continuous Improvement into the ongoing management of the organization.

"No, no," replied Carl. "The parts are more like a backbone—necessary to keep us upright. There is some flexibility in how we perform each part, but we do have to address each one of them; none can be ignored or the whole effort will fall apart. Are there any other questions?"

Jim, the marketing manager, followed right along. "You haven't said anything about problem solving. From what I've heard about Continuous Improvement, I thought that was the heart of the effort."

"It is," said Carl, "but we won't get to it for about ten weeks. At that time, the first-level CITs will become problem-solving teams for fifty minutes a week.

"The top- and mid-level CITs never actually become problem-solving teams. Instead, individuals from these CITs are assigned to cross-functional teams that are formed to solve a particular problem or opportunity. Generally everyone will put in two hours per week—part managing the process and the rest actually solving problems. I'll go into a bit more detail on this next week."

"Part 9 says 'train everyone in problem solving.' How do you propose to do that?" asked Bill, the operations manager.

"We'll start when we've decided this method is a go and the trainers are trained," said Carl. "Then everyone in the organization will attend two workshops, two months apart, in basic problem solving. We already have the manuals for the workshops, including instructions for the trainers."*

"Where do these legendary two hours per week come from?" asked Moe, the new products manager. "Is the stork supposed to deliver them?"

"And is *that* enough time to establish this thing and get any meaningful results?" added Bill.

"Look," said Carl, "from what I've heard, two hours a week to start off will get the job done. Later on we won't have a time guideline as such, but we'll put in whatever time is necessary to get the tasks done by specific dates. After all, we're going to be at this forever. The idea right now is to get started at this pace and see what happens.

"If there are no more questions, we can all go, but before we do, just let me say this. Before we commit ourselves to go ahead with this, we all have to be together on it, and the only way we're going to do that is to learn about this stuff taking it one week at a time. I know some of you are champing at the bit and ready to start tackling problems right now, but you're going to have to wait a while. We're going to spend whatever time is necessary to convince all of us that this is the way to go. That could take as long as three months, but they will be three months well spent.

"That's it for now. We'll get together again next Wednesday at the same time for one hour. Carol will bring in her organization chart, and we'll continue to learn about the method."

---

* The books Carl is referring to are *Trainer's Problem-Solving Manual for Kick Down the Door of Complacency* and *Participant's Problem-Solving Manual for Kick Down the Door of Complacency*.

WEEK 2

- ## More on getting started
- ## More on who does what

Early the following week, Carl and Harvey met in the cafeteria for a cup of coffee. Harvey had been retained as a consultant by Clear Run on a part-time basis for more than eight years. During that time he and Carl had become good friends, with Harvey often acting as Carl's mentor and confidant. They often got together like this to discuss the inner workings of Clear Run, but the topic of conversation today was Continuous Improvement.

"I know Carol's not with me on this," said Carl, "and I sense there might be some resistance from Moe and Nick. What do you think?"

"I think you're right," said Harvey. "From my experience, I've found Continuous Improvement goes in much more easily in areas that are involved in routine work such as production, rather than the nonroutine work such as new product development, marketing, and sales. It also goes in more easily when leaders of departments are not sinking under other major tasks. What you need is someone like Ferg to help you out."

"I really can't spare Ferg to do this," said Carl. "He's already got a huge job directing human resources, information technology, facilities, legal, product scheduling, and strategic planning. I was thinking about you. Could you spare a couple of hours a week to act as our coach?"

"Sure, but I'm no expert on Continuous Improvement."

"I don't need an expert. I just need a person with some savvy."

Quite coincidentally, Ferg dropped in to see Carl later that day. Though he hadn't shown any signs at the meeting, he was obviously concerned.

Carl had had other bright ideas in the past, and they had gone down in flames.

"This Continuous Improvement announcement was a little sudden, wasn't it?" said Ferg. "I mean, we haven't even explored any of the alternatives."

Ferg had always been a big help to Carl. He was one of the most senior people in the organization with the most years of service and, at one time or another, he had gained experience in practically every function in the company. When he spoke, Carl listened.

"Ferg, you're right; I probably should have talked to you before I got the staff involved. But I firmly believe this is the way to go."

"But we don't even know if this is the right approach to take."

"Well," said Carl, "why don't you look into some other approaches? If you find a better way, we can always change. Right now, we're just on a fact-finding mission, if you will. I'm pretty sold on the idea, but we're not going to actually start until there's a consensus to start."

Carl launched the second meeting of his CIT with an apology of sorts. "Since we last met, Ferg gave me a rap on the knuckles about selecting a method to use without due consideration. I guess I'm like a kid with his nose pressed to the door of a candy store. When the door swings open, he dashes in and starts eating. I've learned a lot about Continuous Improvement, and I'm convinced that this is the best approach. You might say the door to the candy store just opened for me.

"Just to be safe, however, I've asked Ferg to do some research on what other methods are out there. He'll report back to us in a couple of weeks. I've also asked Harvey to help us out on Continuous Improvement, and he'll be attending our meetings on a regular basis. Are there any more questions or comments before we get started?"

After a slight hesitation, Jim piped up. "I've got to admit," he said, "that even though I've heard a lot about Continuous Improvement, I honestly don't know exactly what it is."

"I'm glad someone had the courage to ask," said Carl. "It's basically just another name for TQM, which, in and of itself, doesn't mean that much because each practitioner defines the term as he or she sees fit. In our case, however, Continuous Improvement is a method involving everyone in the company in solving operational problems and achieving operational opportunities by continuously improving work-flow processes—the key phrases being *involving everyone* and *improving work-flow processes*."

"Well," said Jim, "I'm so anxious to do *something* that I don't care what we call it as long as we do it. I've been here a long time, and even though we've tried, nothing has really improved in the way we treat customers, especially with our horrible delivery record, which should be called 'never on time.' I know the new order-to-shipment tracking system is coming, but so is Christmas!"

"Right on," said Bill. "For months I've been catching hell for poor products going to customers, when the source of a lot of the problems is in the *design* of the product. I think the companywide approach is the only way to go."

Carl could see that Carol was itching to add her opinion to the discussion.

"Okay," she finally said. "It's my turn. I can see how this will be good for the company and that if we do decide to do it, we should *all* do it. I just don't see how it is going to apply to the sales department. I think having *anyone* in my department spend two hours a week on this stuff is ludicrous!"

Bill broke the silence that followed. "That's all very interesting, Carol, but tell us how you really feel." Even Carol had to laugh at that.

"Well," said Carl, "now that you've gotten that off your chest, why don't you show us that chart you've been working on (see p. 16)."

Carol stepped up to the easel and uncovered her schematic. It was clear that, despite her busy schedule, she'd found time to put in her two hours for the previous week. The display was impressive. It covered the top-level team and everyone involved in sales from Carol on down to the most recently hired sales clerk.

"It's all yours," she said to Carl, taking her seat.

"Great," said Carl. "Each triangle represents a team that will meet once a week to manage the process. We're up here," he said, pointing to the top triangle, "the executive CIT. We will meet weekly for one hour, with me as the leader. If I'm out of town, you will still meet. As long as you're not traveling, attendance is required. There will be no substitutes.

"Our job, primarily, will be to design the method based on the fifteen parts I gave you last week. Basically we will be deciding exactly what to do and when to do it. A couple of the parts might require a temporary specific action committee. If that's the case, I'll appoint one of you as the leader. Other than that, our job will be to delegate most of the installation and operation down through the organization.

"For example, after an executive CIT meeting, Carol will go back to her office and hold the sales CIT meeting for thirty minutes with her staff." Carl pointed to the second triangle on the chart. "She will tell them what we have discussed in our meeting and what actions we are going to take. They'll tell her their concerns, which she will bring back to the executive

Organization Chart for the Top-Level CIT and Carol's (Sales) CITs

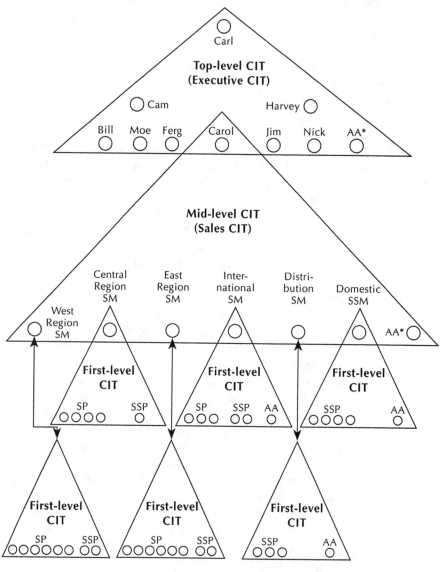

SM = Sales manager
SSM = Sales service manager
AA = Administrative assistant
SP = Salespeople
SSP = Sales servicepeople
* = Not active member of the CIT

CIT meeting the following week. Their primary task, however, will be deciding how to install and operate Continuous Improvement specifically in the sales department.

"After the mid-level CIT meeting, each of Carol's staff people will hold a ten-minute meeting with their first-level CITs to talk about the operation of the method. Once most of the members of a first-level CIT have attended the first problem-solving workshop, that CIT will start meeting for one hour instead of just ten minutes, using the balance of the time in actual problem solving. They will spend their second hour on individual assignments."

"When do we start?" asked Ferg.

"Right now," said Carl. "There's no point in waiting. We don't need to refer to them as CITs just yet; in fact, let's not until we actually agree to start. But I do think everyone needs to know what's going on. So the purpose of these meetings, for now, is to tell people what we are up to and to listen to their ideas and concerns."

"Now remember," said Carl, "the top- and mid-level CITs don't actually *solve* problems. The bulk of that is handled by the first-level CITs. However, you're not going to get off the hook, because each and every one of you is a candidate for a cross-functional team, or CFT—that is, a temporary team formed to solve a problem that involves three or more units or departments. So don't worry, you'll all get a shot at a little problem solving."

Carl knew it was time to wrap things up.

"I'd like Cam to please take minutes of our meetings—no more than two pages—and get them out to everyone here within twenty-four hours by mail or e-mail. The rest of you can use the minutes in your meetings as if they were your own notes. In the meantime, here are a few guidelines for you to follow." He passed out a preprinted sheet of paper (see p. 18). "It's basically everything we talked about last week and today.

"Next week we'll be discussing why we need Continuous Improvement, so I'd like each of you to think about all the ways your time is wasted during the day or week and put some thought into problems we should fix and opportunities we might seize. Ferg, I know you're busy, but I'd like you to put together a questionnaire that we could distribute to everyone else in the company. Ask questions that will help us identify some of the problems out there. You will also need to figure out a way to get everyone in the company to respond.

"The rest of you should make your own organizational schematic like Carol did. And don't forget, mid- and first-level CITs start meeting now. That's it. See you next week."

Continuous Improvement Organization

Refer to the units in the company, when they are working on Continuous Improvement matters, as CITs (Continuous Improvement Teams).

To manage Continuous Improvement:

▪ Top-level CIT meets	Sixty minutes a week	To design and delegate the installation and operation of Continuous Improvement
▪ Mid-level CITs meet	Thirty minutes a week	To install and operate Continuous Improvement
▪ First-level CITs meet	Ten minutes a week	To operate Continuous Improvement

To problem solve and get results:

▪ Top- and mid-level CITs do not actually solve problems, but their members may serve on CFTs—temporary teams formed to solve a specific problem or to achieve a specific opportunity. People in this category spend up to two hours a week managing Continuous Improvement and problem solving.

▪ First-level CITs spend fifty minutes per week in actual problem-solving meetings. Individuals spend up to another hour a week on assignments from their teams.

WEEK 3

■ **Determining the need**

■ **The schedule through week 13**

One week later, as Carl drove to work, he thought about the coming meeting. Carol obviously wasn't sold on Continuous Improvement, but Carl had a feeling she would come around once she understood the breadth and depth of the negative impact that operational problems were having on the company. He'd have to give her another assignment. It would be a good time to reel in Moe, his new products manager, as well. They both needed to see how something done wrong in their departments was impacting the work of people in other departments and throughout the company, and to see how doing their own work more efficiently would help them save time. His plan was to make them and the rest of his team indignant about the current conditions and inspire them with a passion—and a reverence, he thought to himself with a smile—for improvement. If today's meeting didn't do it, perhaps the results of Ferg's survey would. By the time Carl pulled into his parking place, he was ready for the meeting.

Formalities were dispensed with and Carl went straight to the easel, labeling the top of the page "Problems."

"Who wants to start?" he asked.

Moe was first. "Late on new products. Poor cooperation from manufacturing." He was on a roll. "Late financial reports—with errors," he added. "Poor communication between departments. Too long to hire new people." Carl could barely keep up as he madly added each item to the list.

"It takes too long to get help from the computer department," added Cam. "Customer returns for products and credits for sales administration errors are too high."

19

"Salespeople find it very difficult to get product engineers on the phone or to get them to return calls," said Carol.

"Too many meetings," said Bill. "And lousy meetings at that."

"Poor teamwork, high turnover, and low morale," added Ferg.

"Late deliveries. Very few repromises on pending late deliveries. Constant expediting," said Jim.

The list grew rapidly and furiously for thirty-five minutes. By the time they were done, Carl had covered ten sheets of chart paper, yet he knew they had barely scratched the surface.

"This is a good start," he told them, "but I know if we dig a little deeper, we're going to find even more."

"Why would we need any more?" asked Moe. "It looks like we've got enough to keep us busy into the next millennium."

"True, but very few of you mentioned problems that originated in your own areas. And how about problems that are so ingrained, people feel they are a legitimate part of their work—what they are paid to do. Rework is a perfect example. What's worse, we've all come to accept that problems are a way of life—that although we have problems, we are better than we were and no worse than our competitors. As a result, our people have given up calling attention to them because we haven't seen fit to fix them or haven't known how.

"What I'm trying to do now is put these problems and unachieved opportunities into a pile and make that pile so high and so overwhelming that it can't be avoided anymore. So that *everyone* in this room begs me and pleads with me to do something about this awful mess!"

Carl paused, and the room remained very quiet.

"Sorry I got carried away. I'm not mad at you; I am upset with myself for not having done something sooner."

"Nick," said Bill, "do you feel okay?"

"Sure, why do you ask?" said Nick.

"You haven't said anything."

"There's nothing to say; it's all up there," he said, nodding to the chart.

"But you usually have some terse observations. Do you think this stuff is any good?"

"Perhaps for the company, but not for the finance and accounting people."

The silence was broken by Carl.

"Ferg," he said, "are you ready with your report?"

"Yeah," said Ferg, snapping to attention. "I think we should survey 20 percent of the people in discussion groups, having each person here lead at least one of the discussion groups in his or her department. That way, I think, people will start to see that *we're* committed to this thing, and we'll also be getting our information straight from the horse's mouth, so to speak. I'll find leaders for the balance. If we include ten people per session, we will need fifteen sessions."

"How are we going to hit the other 80 percent?" asked Jim.

"We can get them with the written survey. Here's the questionnaire I've prepared (see below)." With that, Ferg handed a copy to each person in the room.

"As you can see, it's pretty straightforward. It shouldn't take more than thirty minutes to fill out. I thought we could bring everyone from a single unit or department to the cafeteria to do it all at once. If we get started

---

A Survey for Everyone

1. Please list all the problems that hinder you from doing your job correctly the first time. For example: lack of training, poor tools or equipment, poor instructions, out-of-specification materials, lack of materials.

2. How much of your time each day is wasted because of the above?

3. What parts of your job would not be necessary if work coming to you was done correctly, on time, every time? For example: inspections, expediting, rework, time in meetings, issuing credits, rescheduling work, arguing with people.

4. What should be done to improve your unit, department, or Clear Run?

Unit or department _____   Date _____

Name (optional) _____

---

right away, I can probably tally the results from this and the discussion groups and report back here in week 7."

"Why do we need the discussion groups *and* the written survey?" asked Carol.

"Well, I actually think the discussion groups will be more productive, especially if people have any difficulty understanding the meaning of the questions and the questionnaire. I also have a feeling that people will feed off each other and things will come out in conversation that simply won't in a written survey. On the other hand, the written survey, which can be turned in anonymously, may get at some subjects that people aren't willing, or are even afraid, to discuss.

"If everyone agrees," said Ferg, "I'll work out the logistics of the discussion groups—who, when, where—and get back to you."

"Sounds good to me," said Carl. "Now, in my efforts to dig even deeper, I'd like you, Carol, to please gather together all the sales complaints you've received in the last two months. And, just to make sure no one thinks I'm picking on Carol, I'd like Cam to compile all the data he has on Clear Run's internal and external quality and reliability levels. I'd like both of you to report back with that information in week 7."

"Whoa," said Bill, who had been with Clear Run for three years and had extensive operational experience with two Fortune 500 companies. "All we have so far are a few glimpses into the method of your madness. Do you have a road map with milestones and time goals?"

"Sorry, Bill, I should have shown you that," said Carl, stepping back to the easel and uncovering a new list of the fifteen parts, with week numbers instead of part numbers (see p. 23). "We already understand the method, and today we started to determine the need. Next week, which will be week 4 of the effort, we'll adopt the four principles. The week after that, we'll fit Continuous Improvement into our four-year plan, and so on, down to week 9 when we'll start collecting problems and opportunities.

"By week 10 we should have all the facts that will allow us to make a decision about whether or not we're actually going to go ahead. If so, we'll start talking about the problem-solving training in week 11. Then, in week 12 we'll prepare for a kickoff meeting where we formally tell everyone in the company about what's going to happen with Continuous Improvement. The actual kickoff will be in week 13."

"So we're not doing a part a week," observed Bill.

"Hell no," said Carl, "I haven't lost all my marbles. As we get going, some parts may stretch over several weeks, such as the assignments I gave

Timeline for the First Thirteen Weeks

Week	Subject
1 and 2	Understand the method.
3	Determine the need.
4	Adopt four principles, and look at the benefits of Continuous Improvement.
5	Fit Continuous Improvement into our four-year plan.
6	Establish formal and informal communications.
7	Examine the resistance to change.
8	Form a vision of what would be going on in two to three years if problems were fixed and opportunities were achieved.
9	Collect problems and opportunities through surveys.
10	Come to an agreement to do Continuous Improvement.
11	Start the problem-solving training.
12	Prepare for the kickoff meeting.
13	Hold the kickoff.

Ferg, Carol, and Cam. This just tells us when we'll begin working on each of the parts; how long they each take depends on the need.

"Next week we will talk about the four underlying principles we need to employ to change the attitudes of people and to make Continuous Improvement work. We will also discuss some of the benefits of Continuous Improvement. So, in addition to meeting with your respective CITs, I'd like you to spend a little time thinking about what we might gain from all this.

"That's it. See you next week."

WEEK 4

- ■ **Adopting the four principles**
- ■ **Benefits of Continuous Improvement**

As this team filed into the conference room the following week, Carl was busy writing on his chart paper. He had spent a lot of time thinking about principles that he and the rest of the company could adopt. The problem had been narrowing them down so there weren't so many that no one would remember them all, at the same time keeping them simple so that everyone could embrace them. It had been some time in the works, but he was sure he finally had them. Four little gems. Four little rules that everyone would remember and live and work by: *Think work flow. Improve daily and relentlessly. Delight your customers and clients. Do things faster.* Unfortunately, they would be hollow unless they became part of everyone's actions. He just hoped his team was ready.

Once everyone was seated, Carl pointed to the first page (see p. 26) and began.

"Think work flow," he said. "All operational work in an organization should be considered part of a work-flow process. Work goes from one person to another person to another person—whether it is taking an order from a customer; manufacturing a part; or packing, shipping, and billing products. People are involved in work flow in three ways. First, they are the recipient of someone else's work—they are a customer, so to speak. Second, they do some work on what they receive. And third, they supply a product or service to someone else—they become a vendor. For example, a sales serviceperson requests and receives samples from a technician and then packs and ships the samples to a customer. That's a work flow.

"Some work flows are short," he continued, "such as the one I just described. But some are long and involve many people. For example,

---

The Four Principles of Continuous Improvement

1. Think work flow.
    - Each person has a mutual agreement with his or her suppliers and customers on the work to be done.
    - Each person performs according to that agreement.
    - Each step in the process is designed to meet the product or service requirements with no waste, no delay, and no unnecessary steps.

2. Improve daily and relentlessly.

3. Delight your customers and clients.

4. Do things faster.

---

obtaining an order for a special product to be manufactured, entering the order, having it scheduled, purchasing the necessary materials, manufacturing the product using a number of departments, shipping it, billing for it, and collecting the payment is one work flow, but each person involved in the process is alternately a customer, a doer, and a supplier.

"Now," he said, "there are three conditions that superb work-flow processes contain. One," he began, pointing to the first item under work flow, "each person in the process has a mutual agreement with his or her suppliers and customers on the work to be done. Two, each person performs according to that agreement. And three, each step in the process is designed to meet the product or service requirements with no waste, no delay, and no unnecessary steps.

"Our job, then, is to make sure everyone fully understands the requirements of the job to be done and to get from them a promise: 'I will always do what I say I will do.'

"We also have to make sure that everyone is involved, because if anyone is left out, some part of some of the hundreds of processes that go on around here every day will not be done correctly or will not be improved.

"Think work flow," he repeated. "The first of our four principles.

"Next," he said turning the page, "improve daily and relentlessly.

"I'm convinced that a large chunk of the brain power in any organization goes unused. People are told what to do. When problems arise, they are generally not solved by the people doing the work. Sometimes managers or supervisors solve them, sometimes experts solve them. But most often problems get patched up, work gets redone, other people do work that another group should have done, and the organization muddles along.

"I think our people *want* to help. They want to make their jobs easier. They want to reduce the foolishness of waste, rework, and nonuseful work. And they want to help the customers. They have ideas. They have knowledge. And we are going to tap *all* of it.

"The key is to focus people on improving the processes they are part of. Trust that they know more about their piece of work than anyone else in the organization and that they are the only people who can do the job. Remember that the only person who knows if the shoe is tight is the person wearing the shoe."

Pointing back to his chart, Carl said, "Improvement has to be a relentless, daily part of *every* job—a condition of employment.

"Once everyone sees how they fit into the work flow, who their suppliers are and who their customers are, the third principle should be easy to adopt," he said, turning the page once more. "Delight your customers and clients. Deliver the products or services, per their needs, at the lowest possible cost, in the most pleasant and friendly manner possible. Enough said.

"Next," he said, flipping the page again, "do things faster." There was a collective groan from everyone in the room. "I know. I know," he said. "You're already working as fast as you can. But I don't want more energy. I want more brain power. I want the waste taken out of the work flow. I want work to be done in entirely new ways that speed up the processes. Speed is the only way we're going to lower costs and beat out the competition. And speed comes from superb processes. So," he said, flipping back to his first page, "back to work flow. Square one.

"Now," he said, looking back at his team, "it's your turn."

The room was quiet while everyone considered the implications. Finally, Ferg spoke up. "Well, I think it's great. Generally when something goes wrong we all ask, 'Who did it?' when we should be asking, 'What in the process went wrong?' We'll eliminate trying to fix personal blame because the fault is in the process."

"I think the work-flow example is pretty static," said Bill. "It's for one particular set of requirements made at one time. In actual fact, requirements from customers are always changing because they want different things or want improvements in what they are purchasing. Let's be sure that everyone understands that, because it means that improving processes will always be with us."

"Being a hierarchical organization," added Harvey, "you have always thought and acted vertically, and mostly top down—not bottom up. But if you adopt the think-work-flow principle, you will start thinking and acting horizontally. It will give you the ability to handle changes in a world that is growing smaller and smaller and has a greater variety of customers and more and tougher competition."

"Harvey's right," said Moe. "Continuing to operate with only a vertical emphasis does not give us a snowball's chance in hell of becoming highly successful."

"Personally," said Jim, "I like the principle of delighting customers and clients. Most of you have seen the sign in my office: 'To sell John Smith what John Smith buys, you must see the world through John Smith's eyes.' Now, if we can just get everyone to see that John Smith represents their internal customers—that is, the people who receive the products of their work—we've made great progress. Then if everyone would treat their internal customers the way they would like to be treated by the merchants who separate them from their hard-earned money, we'd be on easy street."

"I'd like to add two principles from TQM," said Cam. "I'd like to stress prevention of errors and drive toward having no defects."

"That's a good idea," said Carl. "But I really want to have just four. Why don't you find a way to work them in as we go along and certainly when we get to the advanced stage."

Cam grumbled, "If that's all I can get, I'll take it. But believe me, these two concepts are very important."

So far Carl hadn't heard from Carol, which was unusual, but he could see she was thinking. When the discussion quieted down, she finally spoke up.

"I recently had a set-to with the purchasing chief at WorldWide. She really worked me over, which surprised me because we are doing a much better job than we were a year ago. Finally, in frustration, I said, 'Sally, what in hell do you want?' She pointed her finger at me and said, 'When I place an order with you, I want it delivered on time, to the specifications, and to all our other requirements. I don't ever want to hear another word from anyone about that order.' It's going to be tough to 'delight' her, but that's what we've got to do."

Carl could see that Moe was also itching to speak. "Is something troubling you?" he asked.

"I guess I am the skunk at the garden party," said Moe. "I can't disagree with what you want to accomplish, but two hours a week from everyone? Can't we do this some other way? Aren't there any alternatives? I'm concerned about loading any more on people in my department who are *already* overloaded."

Carl was considering how to respond when Bill broke the silence.

"We're all busy, Moe—maybe not as busy as you, but plenty busy. Maybe there are some quick ways all of us could eliminate some wasted time right off the bat. Overworked people are often people who are working inefficiently."

"You may be right. But I'm still not convinced."

Carl half expected Nick to speak out as well, as he was quite sure Nick, who had said nary a word at any of the meetings so far and looked positively bored now, was not with him. He gave Nick a few moments to speak up, but when he didn't, Carl continued. "Maybe it would help if we talked a little about some of the benefits we might start to enjoy.

"Imagine the savings we will realize if defects or errors can be lowered on a particular product from 1,000 parts per million (ppm) to 100 ppm. If wasted resources could be reduced from 20 percent to 2 percent. If the time required to do a task could be reduced from ten days to one day. These all represent a tenfold improvement in performance and are very doable with processes that have not really been worked on."

"Over what period of time?" asked Carol.

"I've been told we can expect these numbers in less than three years," said Carl.

"Take it one step further and you'll see that when product defects are reduced, for example, there will be increased customer satisfaction that, no doubt, will lead to increased sales; time that was wasted dealing with the consequences of poor work can be turned into productive time instead. Managers previously frazzled putting Band-Aids on day-to-day problems can focus on introducing new products and services faster or helping people as individuals. Those whose performance is now considered poor—only because they are working with wretched processes—could get promoted.

"But the most amazing thing is that through the simple activity of having everybody solve the problems involved in their own work, self-esteem will become enhanced, jobs will become more interesting, and each person will have a much better chance of fulfilling his or her own aspirations. Barriers between units will break down as people start to talk to and trust each other, because they are now solving problems together. There will be fewer hassles, arguments, and frustrations, and the right hand will know what the left hand is doing. People will become more helpful to each other and more loyal to the organization.

"That's not all. Suppliers, when treated decently, will become more and more helpful to us. We will be much better able to handle the faster and faster changes on the horizon such as customers who are more demanding, tougher competition that is expanding worldwide, new technology, and a more educated and demanding workforce.

"Everyone in the organization and everyone associated with the organization benefits. Employees, customers and clients, suppliers, owners or trustees, patrons, and the community—everyone."

When Carl was done, some of those in attendance wondered whether applause was in order. Fortunately, Moe broke the silence.

"That's pretty impressive, but do you really think Clear Run will see a tenfold improvement in three years?"

"I do," said Bill. "We only just put a team together to improve the quality and reliability on our engine-control part and already the defect levels have been reduced by a factor of ten. We're so confident that we just signed up with the customer to reduce them another ten times. That's a hundredfold improvement. Given that, a tenfold improvement company-wide seems pretty realistic."

"Well," sighed Moe, "if we can get into that ballpark, it certainly might be worth the time and effort, but I'm still not convinced it's the thing for us to do now."

"We'll put some more meat on these bones in a few weeks when we talk about vision," said Carl. "In the meantime, does anyone have anything else?"

Ferg raised his hand. "I've been thinking a little more about the survey I'm supposed to conduct," he said. "It's going to frighten the hell out of people. They're going to think that we're going to get them to tell us what all the problems are, get *them* to fix them, and, once the problems are fixed, fire a good chunk of them. They're going to think we'll be driving home in our shiny new cars while they walk to the unemployment office. We need to give them some kind of assurance that they're not going to lose their jobs."

"Good point," said Carl. "Perhaps you could draft a letter to the contrary to include with the survey. Why don't you do that and bring it by my office on Wednesday so we can go over it."

Ferg nodded.

"If there's nothing else, I'd like to make a few assignments. Jim, I'd like you to head up a specific action committee to work on communications—that is, communicating our Continuous Improvement effort companywide. You can pull in whoever you want to work on this with you, but I would like you to be prepared to discuss your ideas with us in two weeks.

"Ferg, Bill, here is a copy for each of you of the training manual we'll be using for the problem-solving workshops. I'd like you to look it over and tell us whether you think this method is going to work for us.

"Meanwhile the rest of you can meet with your CITs to discuss the four principles much the same way we did here. That is, describe the principles and then discuss the implications they will have on the people in each unit. The problem-solving workshops will not include a discussion on the principles.

"Next week I will present Clear Run's four-year plan. See you then."

WEEK 5

- **The four-year plan**
- **Carl's letter to accompany the survey**
- **CI counselor**
- **Carl visits Nick and Moe about their commitment**

Carl was relieved that no one had asked him anything about the four-year plan because he didn't have a suitable one yet, but he did know who would—K.V., who was in charge of Clear Run's strategic planning. Carl walked straight down to his office after the meeting.

"Listen," he said. "I need a two- to three-page summary of our big, corporate four-year plan."

"No problem," said K.V.

"Yeah, " said Carl, "but I need it suitable to deliver to everyone in the organization."

"Wait a minute," said K.V. "I can't do that. Our four-year plan is extremely confidential. It's got the numbers we've generated, the details of four new product plans, and our pricing strategy."

"I know," said Carl. "I don't need any of that. I simply want to be able to describe the thrust of Clear Run and what we stand for in understandable and compelling ways." He could see an objection coming and decided to head it off at the pass. "It's easy; just answer a few questions. What does the organization do now? What will be happening three to five years from now: what are our goals? What are the financial objectives for the next three to five years? What specific tasks are being done, or must be done, to meet those goals and financial objectives? And what are the visions and values of the organization toward employees, clients, customers and suppliers, owners or benefactors, and the community at large? Easy."

"How soon do you need it?"

"By Friday afternoon. Look, I don't want you to spend more than six hours on it. Just give it your best shot and I'll tweak it to suit me."

By late Friday afternoon, Carl had a summary four-year plan in his hand and took it home with him over the weekend. By Wednesday morning, it was just the way he wanted it (see pp. 33–34), and he had placed a copy at each spot around the conference table so his team members could start reading it as soon as they sat down.

Once they had all had a chance to look it over, Carl took the floor.

"This should not come as a surprise to any of you," he said. "It's a summary of the corporate plan that we all worked so hard on last spring. If we hadn't finished it then, we'd be working on it right now. So we're a little ahead of the game."

"Actually," said Carol, "I've always wondered why we even have a comprehensive four-year plan. I thought maybe it was just to satisfy some bureaucrat or college professor who said we ought to have one."

"I'll handle this one," said Ferg. "I've played a part in doing four-year plans, or whatever they're called, since they first came on the scene. Their basic function is to make sure top management agrees on the purpose, direction, and goals of the organization. Once that's agreed on, management can start immediate action to do the things necessary to meet those goals. At that point, it simply makes sense to tell everyone else what is needed."

"So why does everyone moan and groan every time the subject comes up?" asked Cam.

"The complaints are usually centered around the time and energy it takes to put the plans together. People have a tendency to make them more complex than they need to be and to drag them out to eternity, when, in fact, the keys to a good plan are simplicity and expediency. Unfortunately, it takes doing a lot of four-year plans to learn how to do and use them well. I'd say this one is pretty good."

"You know what's interesting," added Bill, looking up from the pages he'd just finished reading, "is everything in this four-year plan is going to benefit by the effort we put into Continuous Improvement. As a matter of

Clear Run's Four-Year Plan

1. What does Clear Run do now?

Clear Run is a wholly owned subsidiary of P.H.C., operating as a separate organization under general policy and guidance from the parent company. Clear Run currently manufactures only in the United States and sells five electronic-component product families worldwide—using its own sales force in the United States and P.H.C.'s sales force in the rest of the world. The U.S. sales force also sells the electronic components manufactured outside the United States by other P.H.C. companies. Clear Run is responsible for the research and development of its assigned product families.

2. What will be happening three to five years from now: what are our goals?

Our current new product, still in development, will increase the number of product families to six. In five years, this new product family will account for 40 percent of our sales. The two product families that are number one worldwide in market share will remain number one and together will constitute 30 percent of our sales. The three product families currently ranked third, sixth, and tenth in market share worldwide will keep those rankings and will represent 30 percent of our sales. In three years we will have a new plant up and running in the Far East to manufacture our new product. A new plant will be built in the United States within five years for the two product families in the number one position. New product research and development will remain the major engine to drive our growth and profitability.

3. What are our financial objectives for the next three to five years?

Over the next five years we will improve profitability from our past five-year average of 8 percent pretax to 10 percent. We will do this by working with our customers to stop the pattern of overbuying during good times and doing the opposite during bad times. Our new product thrust will bring us an additional 2 percent pretax profit in three years, and we will be at 15 percent in five years. At the same time, sales will grow 20 percent per year for the next five years.

Clear Run's Four-Year Plan

4. What specific tasks are being done, or must be done, to meet our goals and financial objectives?

We must do the following:

- Introduce our major new product
- Start and complete the two new factories on time
- Continue to hire good people and reduce turnover
- Effectively sell P.H.C.'s product lines in the United States at the planned selling prices
- Have the order-to-shipment tracking system operating

5. What are the visions and values of the organization?

We will continue to be firm, fair, and friendly to all people at Clear Run. We ask a lot from them, and we want to treat them well. And, remembering that customers are the reason we are in business, we will continue to bring them better products, services, quality, and on-time delivery.

At the same time, we will stay on the cutting edge of technology with up-to-date computers and equipment and up-to-date management methods.

We will be more efficient, with less waste and less delay. We will obey all laws and live up to the ethical standards set by our industry association. We will operate at more than the minimum compliance to good practice of health and safety. And we will continue to be a good corporate citizen in our community.

---

fact, it looks like Continuous Improvement is going to be critical to meeting the goals in the four-year plan."

"That's right," said Carl. "In fact, there is absolutely no sense in doing Continuous Improvement if it doesn't specifically help us accomplish our four-year plan.

"So I take it everyone's in agreement on this and we can present it to the mid- and first-level CITs. If so, let's move on to Ferg and the letter he's written to accompany the survey forms."

"Why don't you read it, Carl, since it's from you," said Ferg.

Carl stood and began.

"This is a memo from me, addressed to all people.

"We in upper management are actively discussing whether we should embark upon a Continuous Improvement effort and, if we do, how we should do it.

"In case you don't already know, Continuous Improvement is a method of solving operational problems and achieving operational opportunities by continuously improving work-flow processes. It involves everyone.

"The benefits we hope to glean from this process are extensive—from higher-quality products produced at lower costs to making Clear Run a better place to work. We're hoping that Continuous Improvement will play a key role in our drive to become not just a good company but a superb company—a great place to build a career and a vital, valued supplier to our customers.

"I earnestly believe that by continuously improving the organization, job opportunities will expand. No one will be asked to leave the company because they helped eliminate or streamline their own job. However, if general economic conditions, competitive conditions, or our own particular conditions put us into a position where we need to have a general force reduction, we will have to have one. That, however, is not our intention.

"Consequently, I hope that each and every one of you will approach the attached survey in the spirit in which it is intended: as a vehicle for taking Clear Run to the next level of excellence."

Carl placed the letter on the table.

"It's signed, 'Sincerely, Carl.' Good letter, Ferg. This should give all of us a basis for answering people's questions about what is going on."

In the few minutes that were left, Carl introduced a new subject, the need for a Continuous Improvement counselor. "I think we are going to need more hands-on help in the form of a full-time person to act as our CI counselor. That should make some of you very happy.

"This person will become a member of our top-level CIT and his or her sole job will be to help us—and everyone else in the organization, for that matter—meet our Continuous Improvement goals. This person should know the organization reasonably well and be able to interact as a peer with the top team members. That means we should be looking for someone within the organization.

"In addition to counseling, he or she will act as a facilitator, coordinator, representative, helper, confessor, doer of certain assigned tasks, and secretary of the executive CIT. The CI counselor might also be assigned to manage the two problem-solving workshops and could become the leader or a member of specific action committees.

"Your assignment for this week is to start thinking about likely candidates for this position. If our organization was a little smaller, I think we might get along with someone part time, but being the size we are, it's going to be a full-time job.

"Now, how are you all doing with your weekly meetings?"

There was a significant pause as Carl looked around the table. Finally, Ferg mustered up the courage to speak. "I don't have a special meeting per se. I just take some time during my weekly staff meeting to talk about what we've talked about here."

"What about your first-level CITs? Are they holding their weekly meetings?" asked Carl.

"I've asked my direct reports to carry the message down," said Ferg, "but I wouldn't bet much money that they are doing it very effectively."

No one else said a word. Carl was visibly upset. For a brief moment, he could see the entire Continuous Improvement effort crumbling around him like a house of cards. He turned to Bill, his arch ally. "*Et tu,* Bill?"

"I'm doing the same thing Ferg's doing," he said, "but one of my middle managers pointed out to me that people on the first-level teams aren't accustomed to holding meetings. They don't even have a place to meet."

"Okay, let's fix that," said Carl. "Listen people. What we discuss here *must* be passed along. Each of you is personally responsible to meet with your mid-level CIT for one-half hour every week—no exceptions. Each member of your mid-level CIT must meet with his or her CIT on down to the first-level CITs. I want everybody to know what is going on. No surprises."

This was a wake-up call for the members of Carl's team. It had been a long time since they had seen him so impassioned about anything.

"I'm sure you all know about the 'Coffee with Carl' sessions I hold with randomly selected people from all parts of the company. I'm going to start holding these sessions faithfully every two weeks and will be *very* disappointed if Continuous Improvement isn't on the tip of everyone's tongue. I mean it."

With the exception of Bill's and Cam's offices, which were in the other building, the offices of the top staff were within two hundred feet of each other. Carl would, from time to time, wander into any one of them for a chat. Since Nick, his financial guru, was still a big unknown, Carl decided it was time to pay him a visit. After a few initial pleasantries, Carl got to the point.

"Nick, what are your feelings about Continuous Improvement?" he asked. "You are quiet to a fault in the meetings and I can't seem to get a grip on where you stand."

Nick took a deep breath and looked Carl straight in the eye.

"This is probably pretty good stuff for the company, but I just don't think it applies to finance and accounting," he said. "I can't for the life of me see how the other people in the company are *my* customers. Accounting is special. We're the watchdogs. We make sure the handling of money and the things that money buys are done according to specific procedures. We have a fiduciary responsibility to the board of directors and that's all."

"Your fiduciary responsibility is only one part of the job," said Carl. "How about helping managers use the accounting numbers to make better decisions? And how about improving the processes within your department?"

"The processes in my department are just fine. They are right up-to-date. Our last auditor's report was as clean as a whistle. And as for us helping people, our door is always open."

Carl persisted. "Are you telling me there's no way you could close the books any faster? That there aren't any errors in the weekly and monthly reports that take up people's time in correcting them?"

"Sure, we could make some minor improvements. What do you think I've been doing with this department since I came here? But we don't need a Continuous Improvement effort to make them."

"Is that how you feel about Continuous Improvement for the whole company?"

"Well," Nick answered, "that's really an operating decision; that's outside of my realm."

Carl had heard enough. As he rose to leave, he issued a parting warning. "As a member of my staff, all the key decisions we make are within your realm. I need your insight, your knowledge, and your judgment to make this thing work, and I expect you to give them."

Carl had just returned to his office when Moe showed up. Busy, as usual, Moe got straight to the point.

"Your new love affair with Continuous Improvement is touching, but I'm still not convinced it's worth the time commitment right now. We have got to get the new product developed, made, and sold. It's vital to our future. But I'm already behind schedule and working my tail off. And now you want me to divert some of my energy and everyone else's to Continuous Improvement just when we shouldn't let one single thing distract us. We're going to have enough trouble meeting our deadline as it is."

Carl sat back in his chair and toyed with his pencil. This was not the indifference he'd encountered in Nick's office. This was a desperate plea for help—the kind of help Continuous Improvement could offer, if only Moe could see it that way.

"Did I ever tell you the story about the traveler in the forest and the woodsman?" he asked. "It seems that once upon a time there was a traveler in the forest who came upon a woodsman felling trees. The traveler took a seat on a fallen log and watched the woodsman for a little bit. After a while he said, 'Hey! If you'd let me sharpen your ax, you could chop down twice as many trees in the same amount of time.' The woodsman replied, 'Oh, I can't stop now. I'm way behind already.'

"I know you are busy and your people are even busier. But we have to change some of the practices, procedures, institutions, and principles of the entire organization to make sure the bind you're in right now doesn't happen again. That can only be done if the whole staff, including you, pulls together.

"I'm not asking for any more than two hours a week from you on this, and in the end we'll all get a net savings in time. We could even get this new product out *ahead* of schedule."

"That I'll have to see to believe," said Moe.

"Then my job is to make you a believer," said Carl.

Moe had attacked the ramparts and they held firm. Carl had shown he really wanted the effort, and Moe was, deep down inside, a team player. It was time, Moe decided, to get on the bus. As he headed toward the door, he told Carl, "I'll schedule a meeting with my mid-level CIT this week as you have requested. But I'll wait, along with you, until all facts are in before *I'm* in 100 percent."

Carl was pleased. "You'll see, Moe; it'll be worthwhile to your group right from the start."

WEEK 6

- **Carl's reasons for delaying the announcement to start**

- **Having vibrant communications**

- **Definitions of culture change and change process**

Carl had invited Jim to the cafeteria for a cup of coffee so they could discuss Jim's ideas about communications before the weekly meeting. But Jim, who had been a fixture in Clear Run's sales and marketing operations for a number of years, had something else in mind.

"I need to get something off my chest," he said.

"I'm all ears."

"You are talking and acting as if the decision to do Continuous Improvement was already made, yet you haven't come right out and said it. What's going on?"

"I suppose I do come across as being sold on the idea," said Carl, "since deep down I really want to do it. But at the moment I am still only 95 percent convinced.

"When we all understand what this is about by being immersed in it, when I have all the facts necessary to make a decision, and when I hear from Ferg about alternative methods, then maybe I'll be in 100 percent. If not, it will be time to start paying some attention to the naysayers."

"When will you—or we—make a decision?" asked Jim.

"We'll have all the facts and enough exposure within the next four weeks," said Carl. "I'm not going to have a vote and count ballots, but I do want a strong consensus from the staff that Continuous Improvement is the right thing to do."

"I buy that," said Jim, "but I think you better tell the staff what you just told me."

"Is this my first lesson in communications?" asked Carl. "Now I know why I chose you for the job. By the way, who do you plan to put on your communications specific action committee?"

"That's a no-brainer," said Jim. "The head of public relations and the editor of the *Clear Run Newsletter* for a start. I also thought about asking Darryl, the head of human relations. He's more hard-nosed than Ferg, who's kind of warm and fuzzy, so I thought he'd be a good counterpart. His attitude is, basically, that people have a job to do, and if they can't do it, get somebody who can. But he also has the pulse of people's feelings, so I think he'd be good to have on the committee. Then Elaine, from accounting, got wind of all this and she asked to join as well."

"Elaine! So she's showing some interest," said Carl. "Well, your team sounds good. When are you going to start meeting?"

"I have called our first meeting for tomorrow, so I should be able to report on our discussions at this week's executive CIT meeting."

True to his word, Jim was ready at the next meeting, but before he could make his presentation, Carl took a few moments to explain to the group, as he had already explained to Jim, why he wasn't quite ready to leap with both feet into Continuous Improvement—just yet, anyway. He did, however, promise to involve the group in a decision, one way or the other, before the end of week 10.

That seemed to satisfy everyone, though Carl couldn't help but notice that Nick remained indifferent. "Never mind," thought Carl, as Jim got ready to start. "I'll deal with Nick later."

"During the first meeting of the communications specific action committee," Jim began, "we simply discussed all the things Clear Run is currently doing in formal communications—things such as Carl's quarterly talk to the organization; the monthly policy meetings where managers talk to all their people about what is going on; the *Clear Run Newsletter*; the advertising, publicity, and public relations efforts; and the spotty use of bulletin boards."

"Don't forget the 'Coffee with Carl' sessions," interrupted Ferg.

"Right," said Jim, "and the 'Coffee with Carl' sessions. Then we dove a little deeper into the underlying concepts of formal and informal communications and distilled it into something I'd like to go over with you now." Jim cleared his throat and referred to his notes again.

"People have a deep thirst to know what is going on," he said, "especially, how it will affect them as individuals. If they're not told, they'll spend a great deal of time taking bits of information from here and there and speculating about their futures. People also have a great need to be listened to about their own problems and accomplishments. They need to know that somebody cares, that if they are asked to do something, someone actually cares that it gets done. That's what communications is all about.

"But what Carl has asked for is *vibrant* communications—communications that take into account that each person hears and absorbs information in ways that are unique. It takes some people quite a few doses of the same message to hear and understand it. Therefore, messages must be delivered in a variety of ways, and they must be delivered repeatedly and frequently. This does not have to be long, loud, or expensive, but it must be active and meaningful.

"In regard to our Continuous Improvement effort, we did make four decisions. One, there will be a newsletter specifically for Continuous Improvement, along with bulletin boards. Two, within three weeks of the announcement that Clear Run will be doing Continuous Improvement, there will be a big-time kickoff event. Three, Carl should devote the first half of his quarterly talks to the organization to Continuous Improvement items, and the entire talk should be videotaped so that everyone can see and hear him. And four, there should be an annual party to celebrate the progress we've made and to focus on the future."

"Sounds like there's going to be a whole lot of partying," said Cam.

"We hope so," said Jim. "And there's one more thing. We all decided that it was pretty important for the top-level team to issue some kind of commitment statement that we will communicate to the troops. I'll draft that for us and bring it for review in a few weeks."

A sense of relief washed across the room as each person realized that he or she would not have to write the statement.

"Thanks, Jim," said Carl, getting ready to take the floor again, but Jim held up his hand.

"I'm not through yet. We've just talked about formal communications. Now let me give you our views on *informal* communications, which is all about management talking and listening.

"I think we do the top-down communication—that is, the talking aspect of it—fairly well; I'd give us a 'B' on that. However, we don't always have our receivers turned on, and if they are turned on and we hear something we don't want to hear, we don't do much about it. Good listening is tough, very tough. If you're like me, whenever someone else is talking I'm thinking about what I'm going to say as soon as I can interrupt. Not good! Therefore, on bottom-up communication, I would give us a 'D.' What we need to do is to bring both top-down *and* bottom-up communication to an 'A,' and we can accomplish that pretty well during our thirty-minute weekly mid-level CIT meetings and the ten-minute first-level CIT meetings. What we say here must be taken down through the organization to everyone. By the same token, what our people are saying in the first- and mid-level meetings must get passed back up the ladder to us, here, in the top-level CIT.

"Remember, Continuous Improvement will always be competing for people's attention and affection with all the other things we, as managers, talk about and spend time on. Consequently, the importance of Continuous Improvement in their eyes will depend on how much time they see us spending on it and talking about it.

"So, once we get started, at the close of every meeting or whenever you speak to somebody, find a way to mention Continuous Improvement. You might ask what they think about the latest accomplishment, or how they are doing with internal customers, or whether they've solved all the hindrances involved in their job—anything to let them know that we are fully committed to this thing and that we expect them to be the same.

"As time goes on, we can add questions about communications and, especially, listening to any survey of people's opinions about Continuous Improvement. We should probably even include it as part of our individual performance reviews.

"Before I close, there's one more thing I want to say. Communications should *reflect* the style of the organization, not *form* the style. And communications should not promise the future so much as report the present—the good *and* the not so good."

Carl was pleased as Jim took his seat. He could see that the message had gotten across loud and clear. Carl then launched into a discussion of what was going to happen next week. "We have a lot to cover," he said. "First, Harvey's going to give us his thoughts on 'resistance to change' because a good deal of our success here will revolve around how well we manage any resistance to putting in Continuous Improvement. That should take about forty-five minutes. Then Ferg will give us the results of the internal surveys, and Cam and Carol will report on the state of our product quality and customer service. That should take another forty-five minutes. So, as much as I hate to do it, we will have to meet for ninety minutes next week."

Moe voiced an objection right away. "Whoa," he said, "this is getting to be a little much. I'm spending half my life in meetings. Why don't we use the first hour of our regular Thursday staff meeting to discuss Continuous Improvement, take the chitchat out of our brought-in lunch, and use the remaining time for our staff meeting?"

The group chimed, "Hear, hear!"

"There's an hour we didn't know we had," said Ferg. "We're already starting to see some benefits from Continuous Improvement."

"Hold it, hold it," said Bill. "We've still got ten minutes left in this hour and I've got a question about two terms that keep cropping up whenever I read anything about Continuous Improvement."

"Shoot," said Carl.

"What does *culture change* mean, and what is a *change process?*"

Harvey raised his hand. "Carl, can I take a pass at this one?"

"Sure," Carl shrugged.

"An organization's culture," said Harvey, "is defined by the ideas, customs, skills, values, emotions, interests, manners, tastes, and ways of thinking, talking, and acting of the people in an organization. The culture changes when some, or all, of these things change. Once we embark on Continuous Improvement, we will, in many ways, change our culture.

"A change process is what happens when an organization goes from one direction to another. For example, an organization that does not involve people in improving their work goes through a change process to get those people fully involved. An organization that is totally concerned with production and low cost goes through a change process to become an organization that is concerned with customer satisfaction. And a regulated business with government-controlled pricing goes through a major change process if it becomes deregulated and has to survive in a free economy.

"Needless to say, some top managements carefully think through the things they will do to make the change. Others just start off helter-skelter and stumble along. Some get lucky and it works. Some get success by lots of energy, time, and persistence. And some simply fail. The fifteen-part method we're planning to use is a good change process for doing Continuous Improvement."

"How do you know this is a *good* change process?" asked Bill.

"Are you challenging a person of great wisdom and perspicacity?" asked Harvey, laughing.

"No," said Bill, "I am challenging you," and everybody laughed.

When they settled down, Harvey said, "Those of you who have studied engineering know that every workable product is built on sound scientific observation. Likewise, organizational behavior scholars have made observations and determined what has to happen in order for a good change process to occur. The fifteen-part method draws on those theories."

"Thank you, professor, that's sufficient," said Bill.

There didn't seem to be any more questions, so Carl proceeded to close the meeting. "One more thing before we go," he said. "In two weeks we'll be discussing vision, and I'm going to need some help on this. Bill, would you lead us through the vision exercise? I have an outline all ready and you can stop by my office later to get it. That's it. See you next time."

WEEK 7

- **Managing resistance to change**
- **Ferg, Cam, and Carol's reports on determining the need**

Later that week, Harvey invited Carl to meet him at a local restaurant for dinner to discuss a few things he thought Carl should be paying attention to. He wanted a setting where Carl was not rushed and would have an opportunity to reflect. Once they ordered their meal, however, Harvey didn't waste any time.

"Carl, we've got some undiscussable subjects that have to be discussed."

"What do you mean 'undiscussable'?"

"Too hot to handle. Subjects that, for whatever reason, are not talked about by you and your staff."

"Like what?" Carl was getting a little defensive.

"Well, like keeping Nick as your numbers guy. Like your controlling nature and, in my opinion, your style of introducing Continuous Improvement."

"What's wrong with my style?"

"Well, for one thing, you've got Carol, Moe, and Nick who are using some pretty loud body language to let everyone know they are not in favor of Continuous Improvement. Your approach has been to persuade them, in essence, by simply starting the effort. There has been no effort by you in the weekly meetings to encourage them to give their points of view and have an open discussion. You seem only to want participation in the decision as long as everyone is going to agree with you."

Carl looked at Harvey, then down at his dinner. "I didn't realize I was doing that. What do you think I should do?"

"You could devote a CIT meeting to encouraging people to express and explore their dissenting views while you keep quiet. Or you could talk to the three of them together and listen, really listen, to their concerns. They might even have some alternative suggestions for improvement that you haven't thought of."

"Okay, let me stew about that. But what is there about Nick that is undiscussable?"

"When Nick came to you three years ago, your accounting was a shambles and the public auditors were close to not giving you approval. Nick fixed all that, but ever since he has not contributed one iota to the organization. I know you know this, and some of your staff know this, but nothing has been done about it."

"Well, nobody has said a word to me about Nick in the last twelve months," said Carl.

"That's my point," stressed Harvey. "Nick has become undiscussable in the eyes of your staff because *you* don't want to hear about it."

"I'm beginning to see what you mean. So tell me something about 'my controlling nature.'"

"This is tougher because it is so ingrained in how we operate with budgets and plans, and reviews and reports, and there's hell to pay if someone misses a number he or she promised to deliver. You hold your managers pretty tightly with policies, practices, and procedures. You form some pretty fixed opinions and then take a pass at selling them to people, and if that doesn't work, you just barge ahead. The problem now is that these kinds of things have become undiscussable because you always think you're right. Consequently, your managers have given up trying to change them for the better."

"You're not supposed to take me out, give me a nice dinner, and then kick the hell out of me," said Carl. "You're supposed to tell me what a fine fellow I am."

Harvey laughed. "If I did that, you and I both know that I'd be looking for other work tomorrow. Just look at this as your personal journey on the road to Continuous Improvement."

"Thanks a bunch. I'll do something about all you've said, but it may take a while."

Driving home that night, Carl thought about the situation with Nick and realized he had been avoiding the issue. He knew Nick should go. He was not particularly helpful to his internal customers, and during his last meeting with Carl, he had given clear signals that he was going to be more of a liability than an asset. Carl had tried counseling Nick and had even offered outside courses, which Nick refused to attend. One of the problems with firing Nick, besides the overall discomfort it made Carl feel, was that there was no obvious replacement for him. To make matters worse, his wife and Nick's wife were close friends. He'd have to give this a little more thought, he decided.

Harvey was first on the agenda at the next meeting, and he launched right into his discussion. He'd done this before—hundreds of times, it seemed. It didn't matter who, what, or when; there was always resistance to change.

"This company has a nice style," he began. "Everyone works hard and there is a nice balance between formal and informal relationships. Firm discipline is tempered with the offbeat, and you do get in some laughs. But Continuous Improvement will bring change, and you are going to lead—and become part of—that change.

"Knowing this company and each one of you personally, I don't believe this will involve a radical change. You won't have to change who you are, but you will have to change what you do.

"To do this, you are going to use a change process—the fifteen parts Carl introduced several weeks ago and has slowly, but surely, been implementing ever since. But this won't be just a stroll in the park. You will be confronted with resistance—resistance to change—from all quarters and for a variety of reasons.

"The hardest thing you may have to face in all of this is simply changing people's habits. We are all creatures of habit. We get comfortable in a routine—the way our workplace is set up, when we get our coffee and how we drink it, how we dress, and where we park our car. After all, we're all human. We would resist changing any of these.

"Likewise, the way we do our job is a habit, and when we are confronted with changing any part of it, we will resist. Consequently, people will start resisting the minute you start to change what they do.

"The four principles are starting to be discussed, and these beliefs are probably falling on some very skeptical ears. I don't know how deep or widespread and in what form the resistance will be, but your job is to be prepared for it, to recognize it, and to remove it, wear it down, or work around it.

"Ironically, the greatest resistance will probably come from people in this very room and other managers and supervisors who already feel overworked and underappreciated.

"One of the things you can do is to help them find the time out of wasted time, much as we found an extra hour in our busy lives for this meeting today. You can also try to convince them to change their priorities so that Continuous Improvement always comes first; something of less importance will simply have to slide."

Harvey then repeated the story Carl had told Moe about the traveler in the forest and the woodsman. This brought a chuckle from everyone in the room, followed by silence as each of them saw themselves as the woodsman in the forest.

"There will also be resistance from first-level people," Harvey went on. "People won't understand what you want them to do, and there will be some who won't understand why they should do it. You're also going to encounter people who don't believe top management can pull it off or has the willpower to carry through. 'After all,' they'll say, 'look how they screwed up the zero-based budgeting thing we worked on two years ago and the elaborate, time-consuming four-year-plan stuff that was going to be our savior last year.'"

Carl put his head down on the table, and Ferg patted his arm in mock sympathy. Lifting his head, Carl said, "Trust me. This time it will be different. Would an old scout lie to you?"

"Yes," said Moe, to which everyone, including Carl, laughed.

"All joking aside," said Harvey "nothing will build resistance as much as you and other managers, wittingly or unwittingly, continuing to do things that keep the old ways alive and well. If you spend more time on other things and show more feelings—anger and delight—with other things, people are going to think those things are more important than Continuous Improvement. If people who aren't doing much on Continuous Improvement get promoted or rewarded or given nice assignments, the others will lose faith. If money is made available to units that don't really need it and is unavailable to units that really do need it, people will stop believing in Continuous Improvement. And if heroes continue to be made of people who go *around* procedures to get things done but no heroes are made of people who quietly change processes and produce more and more with less and less effort, people will stop striving for Continuous Improvement.

"Therefore, each manager's individual behavior—holding the meetings, serving on CFTs, talking about Continuous Improvement, doing what the fifteen parts call for—is critical to overcoming resistance."

Harvey let that sink in for a moment before continuing. "One of the things you will have to watch out for is that once Continuous Improvement gets under way, some people will expect instant pudding—immediate solutions to all their problems. This, of course, is impossible, and when the instant pudding never arrives, resistance will flare up again. You'll start hearing things like, 'See, I told you so. This stuff doesn't work.'

"So beware of promising instant pudding. Promise instead the good old-fashioned kind—many small improvements that, over time, will have a huge impact on the entire organization.

"Now," Harvey continued, "it starts to get a bit tricky. On occasion, you will feel forced to make decisions that fly in the face of Continuous Improvement principles, like using off-specification materials to keep production going, for example, or putting a poorly trained person in a job because the job must get done. When people see this, they will say, 'The bosses aren't serious about this. They talk a good game, but when push comes to shove they go back to their old ways. Why should I waste my time with Continuous Improvement when *they* don't care?'

"When necessity demands you go against good Continuous Improvement practices, tell your people why you're going against them, and then explain how you're going to fix things so it doesn't have to happen again. Apologize to them. It's all about communicating, right Jim?"

Jim nodded in agreement.

"Accept the fact that people will test your resolve," said Harvey. "People will test supervisors, supervisors will test managers, lower managers will test upper managers, and each of you, at one time or another, will test Carl."

Harvey took the stance of someone confronting Carl. "Should I go to my Continuous Improvement meeting," he demanded, "or should I finish this job you've been screaming about for the last three weeks?

"If you stand firm, if you show commitment, the resistance will start to diminish. But if you're wishy-washy, the resistance will persist, and it will make your job harder and harder.

"Now, there will come a time when you will have to decide enough is enough. You will have done everything you can to overcome the resistance of certain people, but nothing, not even individual help, counseling, or training, seems to help. At that point, you've got some tough decisions to make. Those people must be replaced, either by moving them into different positions in the company or by terminating them."

Carl couldn't help but think about Nick.

"I don't want to scare you about this," said Harvey, "but you should be aware of it so you can start thinking of ways to overcome resistance. If you don't, you'll have a much tougher time getting Continuous Improvement started, and it will be that much longer before you can call yourselves successful."

Carl thanked Harvey as he took his seat. He then turned the meeting over to Ferg, who was ready with more ammunition in favor of the need for Continuous Improvement.

"Over the last four weeks," Ferg began, "we have held fifteen discussion groups that were attended, collectively, by 165 people. Another 450 filled out the survey. So, all told, we have information from about 80 percent of the people in the organization.

"The first item on the Survey for Everyone was 'Please list all the problems that hinder you from doing your job correctly the first time.' The top five answers were these: One, wrong or missing requirements—that is, the directions, instructions, or procedures required to do the job correctly were either incorrect or simply not there. Two, unavailable material—that is, the supplies or equipment necessary to do the job correctly, again, simply weren't there. Three, poor planning—that includes schedule changes, interruptions, rework, and changes in requirements. Four, inefficient use of meeting time. And five, poor management—that is, poor decisions, late decisions, no decisions, poor policies and procedures, incompetent supervisors, and poorly trained and inexperienced people to deal with.

"When asked 'How much of your time each day is wasted because of the above?' people answered anywhere from 3 to 60 percent. The average was 26 percent.

"Question number 3: 'What parts of your job would not be necessary if work coming to you was done correctly, on time, every time?' The top answers were rework, inspections, expediting, follow-up, meeting with people to talk about it, and 'wasting time talking about people and units that are no damn good.' That last one was a direct quote," explained Ferg.

"The last question on the survey was 'What should be done to improve your unit, department, or Clear Run?' The results here showed a clear distinction between the discussion groups and the written surveys. The discussion groups were composed of people from individual units or departments, so the participants tended to *talk* about problems related to them rather than give suggestions for improvement overall.

"The written survey, however, was a little more brutal in its criticism of management, and we got such comments as 'management needs to shed its I-don't-care attitude,' 'stop political battles,' 'stop hiring the wrong people and start hiring the right people,' 'enforce discipline,' 'hold people accountable,' and 'develop procedures that would force units and departments to work together.'"

"Are we really that bad?" asked Moe.

"Well," said Ferg, taking his seat, "data don't lie."

Carl said nothing, but nodded to Cam to indicate he should give his report next.

Cam spent about ten minutes showing various charts that graphed quality performance on processes and product families going back three years. Then he summed everything up. "Our rework on products is currently at 12 percent. The outgoing quality level, statistically derived, is 3,000 ppm defective or, stated differently, 0.3 percent defective. Customer returns for products not manufactured to specifications is 0.7 percent."

Cam removed his glasses and looked at each member of the team in turn. "That's too high," he said. "Clear Run is not meeting its customers' requirements for quality. The only good news is that we're doing just as poorly in this area as our best-performing competitors, which means that the opportunities are huge. If we can improve *our* quality, we'll blow them away."

"You know," said Moe, "we've heard all this before, but the fact is our customers are still placing orders with us."

"For now, they are," continued Cam, "but remember Detroit? By the time the top brass *there* woke up, 30 percent of the market had gone to the Japanese, and the Japanese were manufacturing cars in the United States. It's time to wake up."

Carol's report cut right to the chase. She walked to the chart stand and hung a list for everyone to see. Then she proceeded to tick off the problems, one by one. "Thirty-three percent missed shipments to the promise date. Nine percent of repromises missed. Customers never notified of pending missed promises. Paperwork errors leading to customer credits of 1.5 percent. Phone calls not returned the same day. Difficulty contacting Clear Run's product engineers.

"On top of all that," she said, turning back to the group, "those of our top ten customers who have a formal system in place to rate their vendors' performance rate us as poor. The only good news is that none of our direct competitors ranks any higher."

She let that all sink in before continuing. "In good times, supplies are short and customers need us, so we get lots of orders. But in oversupply situations, they give most of their business to their leading suppliers. That is why we have has such large booms and busts. To counter this, we need to give our customers more reasons to buy from us other than just having products available." Finished, Carol sat down.

Now it was Carl's turn. "Is there anyone in this room who doubts that we have a mountain of problems here?"

"Well," said Jim, clearing his throat, "as the little boy said when he saw a pile of manure under the Christmas tree, 'There must be a pony here somewhere.'"

"That's one way of looking at it," laughed Carl. "In fact, that pony might just be the fact that our competitors stink as much as we do. So what we have here is a glorious opportunity to gain market share, grow our business faster, and," he added, nodding to Carol, "smooth out the booms and the busts.

"I know you're all as itchy to start as I am," he continued, "but I think we need a few more facts before we decide for sure. The problems we have identified so far have been gathered with an eye toward simply discovering that we have a ton of them. In that we have been successful. Now we have to add what we'll gain through the orderly use of surveys, and we have got to do it right away if we are to stay on our schedule. Therefore, I'd like Ferg to report back to us in month 9, telling us how we will collect even more problems and opportunities for us to address.

"Meanwhile, Bill will lead us through 'forming a vision' next week. Then Ferg will tell us about some of the alternative methods of doing Continuous Improvement that he's been exploring. All told, next week's meeting will take another ninety minutes, but after that I think we can get back to our schedule of one hour a week."

Carl could see that Bill was anxious to say something. "Bill, is there something you'd like to add?"

"As a matter of fact there is," Bill said. "For next week, I'd like each of you to think about what this organization could look like two to three years from now, when many of the operational problems we heard about today are fixed and we start to achieve some of the tremendous opportunities out there. Think about what you want for the future of Clear Run. Start with the words 'I want,' and finish the sentence. For example, 'I want all our clients to be happy. I want to be appreciated. I want all the waste eliminated from our work flows.'

"That way, we'll be able to work together to create a Continuous Improvement vision of Clear Run's future."

WEEK 8

- **Forming a vision**
- **Alternative methods**
- **Carl's reasons for doing Continuous Improvement**

Bill was first on the agenda, with a full hour to help everyone form a vision of Clear Run's Continuous Improvement future before the meeting would be turned over to Ferg.

"I'd like to start by reading you a short piece from the *San Jose Mercury News*," said Bill. "It's about the U.S. women's Olympic basketball team—the one that won the gold medal in 1996." Bill adjusted his glasses and started to read.

> Teresa Edwards bent her head to receive her gold medal. Then Jennifer Azzi, Lisa Leslie, Sheryl Swoopes, and on down the line. Tara VanDerveer stood to the side and watched, tears brimming in the tough taskmaster's eyes.
>
> She had seen this scene before. Every day in her head, she played it out all the way through the anthem and the raising of flags right down to the hand waves at the end.
>
> She had even seen it in reality. Last Nov. 2, when the U.S. women's basketball team played Georgia at the Georgia Dome, VanDerveer brought her team into the cavernous facility early, lined the players up on what was then the Atlanta Falcons' 50-yard line and had each player try on the gold medals Edwards had won in the 1984 and 1988 Olym-

pics. They played a video with the Olympic anthem. The players cried. Everyone had their picture taken wearing the medal.

"I just told them, 'Don't let anything come between you and a gold medal,'" VanDerveer said.

They didn't. Not Brazil, to whom the U.S. lost in the world championships in 1994. Not competing professional opportunities. Not overwhelming expectations. Nothing.*

"That," he said, "is what forming a vision is all about.

"A vision is a picture of the future—a picture that answers the questions about where we will be two to three years from now. What will people be doing? What will Clear Run's relationships be with its customers and clients? With its suppliers? How will people be dealing with and treating one another? Will our list of problems and opportunities be large or small? How will people feel about working for Clear Run? How will people feel about themselves and their future? Will the organizational direction have been achieved?

"The easiest way to answer those questions is to figure out what we want. It was pretty clear what the U.S. women's basketball team wanted: they wanted that gold medal. But what, *exactly*, do we want?"

Bill flipped the top page of the chart paper to reveal a list he had prepared ahead of time. "Here's a short list of a few of the things I want. I want to cut my wasted time from 25 percent to 5 percent and put the time I save into opportunities. I want to have everyone look forward to coming to work. I want to get close to working regular hours without mindless rush, rush, rush.

"Now, for the next five minutes or so, I'd like you all to jot down what you want. Then you will each choose one item, which we will then try to work into a vision statement."

A few of them scribbled furiously for the next five minutes. The rest stared off into space or down at their papers, carefully pondering. When the five minutes was up, Bill looked around the room and then focused on Carol. "Carol," he said, "let's start with you. What do you want?"

"I want our customers to prefer to do business with us because we are extremely capable in fulfilling their needs." Bill wrote as Carol spoke.

Then it was Cam's turn. "I want to be shipping products with less than 1 ppm defects."

Everyone's jaw dropped. That represented a 3,000-fold improvement.

---

* Ann Killion, *San Jose Mercury News,* August 5, 1996, Special Section 1D. Copyright ©1996 San Jose Mercury News. All rights reserved. Reproduced with permission.

"Aren't you being a little greedy?" asked Jim.

"You asked what I wanted," Cam shrugged. "But if that's a little much, let's make it 2 ppm."

Everyone started to laugh, but they could see he was serious and Bill had already written "2 ppm" on the board.

"Ferg?" he asked.

"I want everyone to feel good about themselves and their future prospects at Clear Run."

"I want new products, lots of them, far ahead of our competitors," said Moe.

"I never want to hear a complaint from a customer," said Carl. "Instead, I want to hear of new ways we can be of help to customers and to receive compliments for what we are currently doing for them."

"You would be difficult," said Bill, who was trying to fit everything on a single piece of chart paper.

"I want to meet our four-year-plan goals," said Nick.

"I want all new products to be out on schedule and to meet our customers' requirements," said Moe, taking a second turn.

"That's what I wanted," said Jim. "Okay, here's another one. I want superb cooperation and teamwork among people and units and departments."

"Harvey?" asked Bill. "We haven't heard from you yet."

"Okay, I want every single person to have earned appreciation for meeting their Continuous Improvement goals."

"I want the time it takes to do things reduced by a factor of ten by eliminating all the waste in our processes," Bill said, adding his own. "Okay. This is a good start—the basis of our vision statement. I'll take this list with me and work on it for awhile. By next week I should have a preliminary vision statement ready for us to review."

"And then what are we supposed to do with it?" asked Moe.

"It should be part of our four-year-plan summary, part of our communications, and a tool to be used by any manager or supervisor with his or her team," said Carl. "I for one would like to see some gold medals worn around here!"

"Thanks, Bill," said Carl. "Ferg, it's your turn. Did you come up with any alternative ways to do Continuous Improvement?"

"Not really," said Ferg. "In fact, everything seems to point to the path we are on, particularly in the area of leadership. The most successful efforts were, exclusively, those that were led by the top person in the organization. And by that I don't mean that the top person simply appointed a committee of 'available' people to lead the effort. Time and again, the results confirmed that this didn't work. Not only that, but when it did fail, it created such a negative impact on people that it was very difficult to restart with an effort that *was* designed correctly. So, in that regard, with Carl's active leadership, we are doing everything right.

"In the course of my research, I did come across some companies that were applying some of the techniques of Continuous Improvement to specific projects, much as we are doing with our order-to-shipment tracking system and engine-control project. They'll probably be successful—for the time being, anyway. The problem is that their success will be limited to those few projects. So, again, I think we're on the right path by expanding our Continuous Improvement effort companywide."

He paused, then said, "Now, for the *really* interesting stuff. Moe, pay attention! Just about everyone I spoke with who has a successful program in place is convinced that they have *made* far more money than they have *spent* doing Continuous Improvement. As far as money goes, the figure that kept cropping up was five dollars saved for every one dollar spent. By 'money spent' I'm referring to out-of-pocket dollars and not the time people have to spend away from their 'regular jobs.' Very few of the people I spoke with have ever had to hire additional people or schedule overtime to make up for the time people spent on Continuous Improvement. And there were no large expenditures that couldn't be fully justified on the normal return-on-investment criteria. One person summed it up pretty nicely: 'Use your brains, not your checkbook.'"

"The way I see it," said Carl, taking the floor once more, "we've got two choices. We can either go ahead with Continuous Improvement with me in charge of applying the fifteen parts to the entire organization, or we can just continue as we have in the past on a project-by-project basis until the time is ripe to do this thing right. The last thing I want to try is a committee-directed effort—that would be a disaster.

"Personally, I think that, if nothing else, the last eight weeks has shown us that we need to go ahead with *something* or we're just going to sink under our own weight. It has also shown us that we *can* find the time to do this and to do it right. Now, some of you have put in some extra time, and I want you—Ferg, Jim, Bill, Carol, and Cam—to know how much I appreciate it. I also want you to know that I haven't been idle all this time."

Carl adjusted his glasses, cleared his throat, and began. "First, let me put Continuous Improvement into the context of the future of Clear Run. The single most important thing we can do to grow and to be prosperous is to supply our customers with new, exciting products and services that differentiate us from our competitors. These, for the most part, are the products from Moe's department—products that must be designed, manufactured, and sold successfully.

"But new products do not, and cannot, live in isolation. New products will take us to the nice part of town to visit, but it's good quality, speedy delivery, and low cost that will allow us to actually live there. For that, we're going to need the input of every person, unit, and department in the company. And that's what Continuous Improvement is all about.

"Now, it turns out that most great organizations share two common characteristics. First, they are led by people with the ability to set a successful strategic course that includes finding growing markets and choosing the right products and services to offer them. Second, these leaders have the ability to get people to execute superbly on all tasks by paying attention to detail and inspiring people to always keep improving—to keep excelling.

"Right now there are three reasons why I want to do Continuous Improvement. The first is the most obvious: to solve operational problems and achieve operational opportunities. The second reason is a little more obscure. I simply want to turn on the sunshine around here—to let people's self-assurance flourish, to make their work more fulfilling, and to let them know that they can go as far as their abilities and desires can take them. The last reason, simply, is to learn the fundamentals of Continuous Improvement so we can take advantage of a whole array of advanced techniques and management methods that can help us be better—things that might otherwise be beyond our reach if we hadn't done the basics first.

"That, in a nutshell, is it, and I think it's reason enough for us to go full-steam ahead. However, before we do, there are a few more things I need to consider and a few people at this table I need to speak with. For the time being, I can promise you that I will come to a decision in two weeks, at which point we'll either agree to proceed or limit ourselves to something less ambitious."

"I'd like to add something here, if I may," said Jim. "I think you should talk to all the people who report directly to us so they can hear, straight from you, what you have just said to us. It might also help you get a sense of their understanding and acceptance of Continuous Improvement."

"How about Monday at 3:30 in the cafeteria?"

"I'll set it up," said Jim.

"Now, last week we compiled a mound of problems," said Carl, "with the express purpose of making us indignant enough to do something about our plight. Next week we're going to start, through surveys and other means, to add to that mound.

"So, there's no homework this week except to take a look at the job description Ferg has posted on the bulletin board for a CI counselor and to let either Ferg or me know if anyone comes to mind. That's it. Let's break for coffee before the regular staff meeting."

The following day, Mary Louise, the project manager on the engine-control project, was standing in Bill's office. "I want the CI counselor job," she said.

"I thought you'd be in to see me," said Bill. "What took you so long?"

"Haste is not dignified."

Mary Louise had joined Clear Run six years ago, right out of graduate business school with an undergraduate degree in engineering. She didn't appear to put in the long hours some of the others did, but when she went home at night her desk was clean and all her tasks were attended to. She was witty, given to strong opinions, and had the ability to take a job and make it happen. Her experience was in product development engineering, but she knew how to treat customers. She was dedicated to delivering products on time, every time, and had little tolerance for wasting time. She was the perfect candidate. Bill had only one reservation. Could he spare her?

"Bill," she assured him, "the engine-control project is in great shape, and my number two person is ready to take it over. Not only that, I'm pretty sure the customer likes her better than he likes me. If I were hit by a truck, you'd put her in my place, wouldn't you?"

"Yeah," said Bill, shrugging his shoulders. "Go for it. Why don't you go see Ferg first, then Carl. And good luck."

WEEK 9

- ■ **Collecting problems and opportunities**

- ■ **Clear Run's vision statement**

- ■ **Carl's visit with Carol, Nick, and Moe about their reluctance to do Continuous Improvement**

That Sunday, Carl sat in his backyard with a tablet of paper and a pencil. All was peaceful and quiet, except for one granddaughter for whom he was momentarily responsible.

Carl had decided that this was the week to confront Carol, Moe, and Nick about their feelings toward proceeding with a full-blown effort. He was still smarting from Harvey's words about how he was handling their disagreement with him. Normally he would have barreled ahead—bullying, charming, and persuading—on a decision like this. But this one was different. The stakes were high. And perhaps their reluctance stemmed from legitimate reasons—reasons they hadn't yet revealed. He decided he would just state his position with no bombast and no baloney and then get them to state their positions and rationales. The question was whether to do this during the next CIT meeting with all the other members present, in a meeting with just the three of them, or with each of them separately.

He doodled on his pad, jotting down the pros and cons of each plan. He decided to see the three of them together immediately after the next CIT meeting on Thursday.

Ferg was first on the weekly agenda. "I have formed a specific action committee to collect problems and opportunities," he said. "The ones we have talked about so far were gathered for the sole purpose of showing us how bad off we are and what opportunities are sitting on our doorstep. Now we must collect even more problems and opportunities using slightly different surveys."

Ferg handed a packet of four survey forms to each person. "Three of the four surveys we've prepared will not only supply information on current problems and opportunities, but they will also give us a means to measure our improvement year after year. I will take care of conducting the two internal surveys (see below and p. 60), running them in much the same way we did the initial survey. But I'd like Bill to take charge of the supplier survey (see p. 63) and Carol to handle the customer survey (see p. 62)."

"No way," Carol practically shouted. "No way will I do a customer survey now. Do you want me to pour gasoline on a fire? Let's do something *for* the customer first, like improve delivery, cut quality returns, and answer their telephone calls. Then I will gladly conduct a customer survey."

Internal Survey of Problems

Please list up to ten operational problems that, if fixed, would make the operation under your responsibility truly first class, thereby delighting internal (inside the organization) and/or external (outside the organization) customers and clients.

Unit or department _____   Date _____

Name (optional) _____

Survey of People's Opinions

Please give your opinion, using the numbers below, on the following items.

1 = disagree strongly   2 = disagree mildly   3 = agree
4 = agree positively   5 = agree strongly

1. I have been well trained and know how to do my job   _____
correctly.

2. I have the tools, the resources, and the time to do my   _____
job correctly the first time, every time.

3. When the processes of my work or the output of my   _____
work does not meet the requirements, I know about it
immediately.

4. I am given the time and the resources I need to con-   _____
tinually try to improve the processes and, therefore, the
output of my work.

5. The people who give me work, supply me with   _____
instructions, inspect my work, and receive my work
know what they are doing.

6. My manager or supervisor listens to me, helps me, and   _____
is friendly while still expecting me to perform well.

7. Finishing work on time while meeting specifications   _____
ranks equally with producing high output and keeping
costs down.

8. What problems do you have in doing your work correctly the
first time?

9. In what ways could the organization be better?

Unit or department _____   Date _____

Name (optional) _____

Customer or Client Survey

Please rate our performance.

   1 = very poor   2 = poor   3 = fair   4 = good   5 = excellent

1. How well do we meet your purchase order in terms of   _____
   quality, reliability, on-time delivery, and paperwork?

2. How well do we understand your needs and desires?   _____

3. How would you rate our competence? Do you think   _____
   we know what we are doing?

4. How would you rate our attitude? Are we pleasant   _____
   and friendly?

5. How well do we respond to your needs?   _____

6. How flexible are we to your needs?   _____

7. Do you have any problems working with us? Please be specific.

8. How may we serve you better?

Unit or department _____   Date _____
Name (optional) _____

"Okay, okay," said Carl. "We can postpone the customer survey for the time being, but I do want Ferg and Bill to report back to this group no later than the end of month 4 with all the other data and information."

Ferg was still reeling from Carol's outburst, but he carried on. "I think Carol and Cam should at least be prepared to update us on our standing with customers and quality at that same meeting. I also think Jim should cover where we stand relative to our competitors."

Next on the agenda was Bill's report on vision. He stood and read each item, one by one, from a sheet of paper.

"In two to three years, Clear Run will be the supplier of first choice for 95 percent of its customers.

Supplier Survey

Please rate our performance on the following items.

1 = very poor   2 = poor   3 = fair   4 = good   5 = excellent

1. How well do our purchase orders state our require-   _____
   ments in terms of quality, reliability, on-time delivery,
   and paperwork?

2. How well do you think we understand what you are   _____
   doing?

3. How well do we know what we are doing?   _____

4. How would you rate how well we express our needs   _____
   and desires?

5. How would you rate our attitude? Are we pleasant and   _____
   friendly?

6. How flexible are we to your needs?   _____

7. How would you rate us in terms of fairness?   _____

8. What needs do you have that we could serve?

9. Please list any problems you have working with us.

Unit or department _____   Date _____

Name (optional) _____

"Most of our people will run—not walk—to work because they enjoy what they do, because it's a pleasure for them to deal with their peers, and because they all feel they have helped themselves improve.

"Everyone will spend some time, daily and relentlessly, improving what he or she does.

"And most of the waste will have been designed out of the work, work will be done faster, schedules and promises will always be met, and everyone will be working on opportunities."

"Not bad," said Carol, "considering you're a manufacturing kind of guy."

"You've almost convinced me," said Moe. "Almost."

"So I gather it's not too unrealistic if we all buckle down and get to work?" asked Bill.

"I don't think so at all," said Carl. "That was a great piece of work. Cam, let's include the vision in the minutes for this week, and Jim, let's include it with our summary four-year plan and use it in all our formal communications."

The meeting was almost over, but Carl had one last thing to add. "Now that we have gathered an obnoxious pile of problems, seen that doing Continuous Improvement will help us meet our four-year plan, envisioned the future with Continuous Improvement, discussed the benefits, and heard from Ferg about alternate methods, it is time to agree on a formal, precise method of actually doing it. That will be the first item on next week's agenda.

"Then, assuming we agree to begin, we'll discuss the commitment statement drafted by Jim and select a CI counselor from a list of very good candidates.

"Let's break for coffee before our regular staff meeting."

Over coffee, Carl asked Nick, Moe, and Carol when would be a convenient time for them to get together with him. They all agreed to meet the following day.

The next day, the four assembled around the small table in Carl's office. "I've made up my mind," Carl began. "I'm 100 percent convinced that we should go ahead, and I believe everyone else on the team is with me. What I want to know now is where you stand."

Carol was the first to speak up. "Carl," she began earnestly, "I know this is essential for the company. It's really a no-brainer. I'll cut my throat if you don't proceed. But, for the life of me, I don't see how it applies to the sales department and how we are going to put in the two hours a week. My main concern is the salesmen who are out on the road and only go into the field offices once or twice every two weeks. I just don't see how we're going to convince them to give us two hours a week."

"Can't you get them involved in some other way, perhaps via telephone?" asked Carl.

"I suppose I could. I just haven't had time to think about how to do it."

"Are those your only concerns?" asked Carl.

Carol nodded.

"Well, look, we aren't going to do anything foolish or anything that would hurt the company. The two hours per week is just a guideline, a parameter. I'm sure we'll be able to work out something to accommodate the salespeople in the field."

"Well, if that's the case, I'm in 100 percent," she said.

Carl turned to Moe, who spoke up right away. "I've got to admit that I had my doubts at the beginning, partly because I've been party in the past to new schemes that have failed. So I kind of took the role of devil's advocate.

"But I'm beginning to see how it might be of help, particularly in my department. For example, these meetings have started me thinking about our major problem of slipping schedules and why that happens and how we can avoid it. As a result, I've decided to engage a consultant in project planning—an expert. In that respect, I've already seen a benefit from Continuous Improvement.

"The upshot is that I'll bite the bullet on the time guideline for my people and forge ahead with the rest of you. Mind you, some of my staff will be kicking and screaming all the way, but the majority are anxious to get going."

"That's a huge relief," said Carl. "I want you to know that I really appreciate your willingness to lead your group into battle and your having the guts to be pessimistic and to make sure Continuous Improvement will be good for all of us."

That left Nick, but before Carl could say anything Nick spoke his mind. "I've got to be honest with you," he said. "I haven't changed my opinion one bit since our last face-to-face. But I'll go along with everyone else, if that's what they want."

It should have been a moment of triumph, but it wasn't. All the way home, Carl thought about Nick and the pros and cons of keeping him in his job. He decided to wait before making a decision so he could talk to Ferg and find out whether Elaine was ready to be promoted.

WEEK 10

- **Coming to an agreement to do Continuous Improvement**

- **Approving the commitment statement**

- **Selecting a CI counselor**

Harvey and Carl were sitting in the clubhouse bar after a Sunday round of golf. "So, now that you have the strays corralled, do you still think you can pull it off?" asked Harvey.

"I'm like that duck moving across the pond out there," Carl said, nodding toward the big picture window in the clubhouse. "I may look carefree on the surface, but underneath I'm paddling like hell. I've also come to the conclusion that it's time for Nick to move on. I just need to discuss a few details with Ferg first."

Harvey said nothing. He knew this had been a difficult decision for Carl.

The following Thursday, Carl called the weekly meeting to order.

"The first item we need to discuss," said Carl, "is whether we are going to proceed with a full-blown effort led by us, or whether we are just going to use some Continuous Improvement techniques here and there. I am obviously in favor of the all-out effort. But I'd still like to hear if there are any serious concerns or objections from any of you or your mid-level CITs."

"I've had our human relations people out and about listening," said Ferg. "The vibes are basically positive, so my CIT is foursquare in favor."

"We are ready and able, too," said Bill. "I'll have some resistance, that's certain, but if we lead this thing properly, I think we'll have a winner. I do, however, think we should clarify a few key phrases before we all hold hands and jump into the water."

"Such as?"

"Such as 'required to participate' and 'spend two hours a week.'"

"Good point," said Carl. "Look, everybody, 'required to participate' means that for any individual, becoming involved and actually solving problems is not optional. People may volunteer for specific assignments, but if they are asked to do something, they are required to turn to the task.

"The 'two hours a week,' as I've said before, is simply a guideline. Everyone is required to participate, but the amount of time they put in is somewhat flexible. Some people, salespeople in the field, for instance, people on machine-paced jobs, drivers, or shift people, might never devote two hours a week. Other people might put in more. The idea is that during any one week, our 750 people will be spending a total of 1,500 hours on Continuous Improvement.

"Is there anything else?" asked Carl.

"Yes," said Moe. "Why are the meetings held weekly?"

"Weekly meetings reinforce the idea that Continuous Improvement is part of the regular routine. When we, as top managers, make it regular and routine, it starts to become a habit. And that's what we want. Again, it's a guideline—a good practice, if you will—to hold these meetings every week at the same time in the same place.

"Are there other concerns or issues?" he asked. Seeing there were none, he said, "Then it's a go.

"Thank you," he added. "I just want you to know that I will lead this with all the wisdom and tenacity I can muster. And I know you'll be enthusiastic leaders in your own areas and will continue to be superb members of this team. Now it seems appropriate to turn the meeting over to Jim, who has drafted a commitment statement for us."

Jim rose from his seat and passed each person a slip of paper titled "Clear Run's Continuous Improvement Commitment (see p. 69)."

"This statement was drafted by the communications specific action committee. It is purposely short and sweet. The idea is for each of us to sign it. Then we will make copies of it for everyone in the company and have some three-by-five-foot posters hung in the lobby of this building, in the plant next door, and at the Concord plant."

Clear Run's Continuous Improvement Commitment

We, the management of the Clear Run Company, are committed to lead in Continuous Improvement.

We will strive to more than satisfy our customers by continuously improving our work-flow processes with help from everyone. We will deliver on time, every time, to the agreed-upon requirements.

_____

President

Quality Manager	Marketing Manager	Operations Manager	Sales Manager
New Products Manager	Finance and Accounting Manager	Administration Manager	Continuous Improvement Counselor

---

"That's great," said Carl. "If anyone wants to make any changes to the statement, talk to Jim after the meeting so he can have the final version to us by next week."

"One more thing," said Jim, "Our committee has been planning a companywide kickoff meeting, to be held three weeks from now, to officially introduce Continuous Improvement to everyone at Clear Run. We'll talk more about this next week."

Next, everyone turned their attention to selecting the CI counselor. Seven people had applied for the position. Ferg felt that only three were serious candidates. The three were pretty quickly whittled down to one, Mary Louise. Not only was she a perfect fit for the job, but she had visited with most of the executive CIT members, including Carl, and requested the job.

"Okay, everyone," said Carl. "The next really big thing we have to do is train everyone in problem-solving techniques so we can start the problem-solving meetings. Remember, the central activity of Continuous Improvement is problem solving. Unfortunately, most people—and our people are no exception—have never received formal training in problem solving, which is just as well, actually, because it's important that we all use the same method and the same language. So, *we're* going to provide the training.

"Now, it's paramount that everyone, and I mean *everyone*—attend," he said, making eye contact with each person in the room. "Since it will be everyone's first belly-to-belly exposure to Clear Run's Continuous Improvement effort, it must be done well. We'll talk more about training and the kickoff meeting next week.

"Finally, before we break up, I want you all to know how much I appreciate your patience with me over the last ten weeks. We are now officially under way, and you all have a green light to tell everyone that it is a go. Together we're going to make Continuous Improvement a huge success."

WEEK 11

- **Elaine promoted**
- **Summary of the training material**
- **Selecting Workshop 1 trainers**
- **Planning the kickoff**

It was time to do something about Nick. Carl walked into Ferg's office early in the week and asked, "If Nick were to disappear tomorrow, would Elaine be ready to take over as head of finance and accounting?"

Ferg dropped what he was doing. "You're finally ready to do something about Nick?"

"Yes, I am," said Carl with a sigh. "I've gone the extra mile with him, and more, but he just doesn't get it."

"I agree," said Ferg. "Let me see what I can find out about Elaine. I'll let you know tomorrow."

Everything Ferg discovered about Elaine bode well for her promotion. She had come to Clear Run about two years ago and was highly recommended by Clear Run's public accountants. Although young, she was well grounded in finance and accounting, but she had little experience in broader management. However, she was very good in dealing with the people in her department and with others in the company. When people asked her for help, they got it promptly. Most importantly, she would be an asset to Continuous Improvement, instead of a liability.

The following day, Nick was given his notice and Elaine became the manager of finance and accounting.

Carl opened the weekly meeting by welcoming Elaine and Mary Louise. Next he thanked Cam for being the interim secretary and relieved him of that task, turning it over to Mary Louise. Then he asked Mary Louise to talk to the group about training.

"Can I just say something before she starts?" interrupted Carol. "I think I'm speaking for everyone here when I say 'welcome aboard' to both of you. We're really glad you're with us."

"You've got to jump fast when Carol is around," said Bill, "but welcome anyway."

"Speaking for myself," said Mary Louise as she stepped to the front of the room. "I couldn't be happier that we've decided to do Continuous Improvement, and I am honored to have been given the CI counselor's job.

"At my meeting with Carl, he gave me the problem-solving training manual to look over. Then I visited with Carl, Ferg, and Bill, who have also read the manual. And we all agree that the method presented is a good one.

"There are basically two complete problem-solving workshops. Everything we need to run the two workshops and teach the problem-solving techniques is right here," she said, tapping the manual in front of her, "including instructions on how to train the trainers.

"In each workshop the participants are taught, through solving a short case, how to select a problem to solve or an opportunity to achieve, how to redefine the problem or opportunity so that it is more narrowly focused and concrete, how to set a goal, how to find the root causes of a problem, and how to remove those root causes and achieve results.

"The first workshop, Workshop 1, takes about nine hours. It involves the Surfside Market, a business with many problems, one of which is solved by the workshop participants. The second workshop, Workshop 2, is designed to take about six hours and should be taken about two months after the first one. In it, Pete builds a puppy pen to please his wife, Caroline, but he builds it *his* way, which is, of course, the 'wrong' way. In this workshop, the participants actually redesign Pete's process of building the pen.

"Both workshops are fun and straightforward. The participants learn how to logically find and solve a problem using twenty-two techniques, such as how to collect data, brainstorm, ask seven pertinent questions, do a requirements analysis, make a cause-and-effect diagram, ask 'why' five times, create a work-flow chart, and measure and display progress toward a goal.

"We'll start selecting the trainers right away and start the actual training in the first week of month 6. If we figure that each trainer should teach

Workshop 1 twice with fifteen people in each session, we will need twenty-five trainers for our 750 people. Once the training is done, each trainer can coach two or three of the problem-solving teams during his or her weekly meetings—let's say for the first year."

Bill interrupted. "How much time will the trainers need to devote to this?"

"It will take about twenty hours of training plus another eighteen hours to teach Workshop 1 twice and ten hours of training and twelve hours to teach Workshop 2 twice. The nice thing is that the trainers don't need any prior experience in either teaching or problem solving. The only thing the job requires is a desire to teach and coach.

"I think we should start with a pool of between thirty to thirty-five people as trainers," she continued, "because surely a few will drop by the wayside as we get under way. So, if it's okay with everyone here, I'll prepare a job description by tomorrow and send you copies. What I need from you is for each of you to please make people available. Ideally, we'll have some names to look at as early as next week and can have all the candidates selected by the end of the following week."

Carl was impressed. Mary Louise had taken the bull by the horns and was wrestling it to the ground.

"You should go see Darryl in human relations," said Ferg. "He can help you post the job description and give you the names of some likely candidates. I think it's important that the trainers come from all parts of the company."

Once Mary Louise sat down, Carl took over again. "Mary Louise, perhaps you should put together a specific action committee on training. It could include Darryl and the top training person from the human relations department. You might also be able to enlist Bill here, who has some training experience. Besides, most of the people in the company are in his area. Cam, I think you should be a part of this as well." Both Bill and Cam nodded in agreement, and Carl introduced the next item on the agenda.

"Jim," said Carl, "you're next. How are you coming with plans for the kickoff meeting?"

"We've been as busy as little bees," said Jim. "I've rented a local movie theater for the kickoff meeting, which will be held two weeks from yesterday from 10 A.M. to 1 P.M. This should cover everyone on the day shift. Then we'll have another meeting that evening in the cafeteria for the people on the swing and night shifts. We'll hold a third meeting in Concord the following day for all the people out there.

"We're still working on the format," he continued. "Right now we're thinking that Carl should open the session and talk for awhile about some of the problems we're facing and the opportunities at hand. Then I think each of us should speak for no more than three minutes each on the benefits that Continuous Improvement will bring to our individual departments. After that, Carl can describe the effort for maybe another twenty minutes and close with lots of time for questions."

When Jim was finished, Carl wrapped up the meeting. "Next week we'll talk more about the kickoff meeting and discuss the selection of trainers. If we have time left over, we can talk about anything else you might need to discuss.

"Before you go, let me just add one more thing. The problem-solving training will make us all better problem solvers. But if there's something that needs to be fixed now, today, or tomorrow, for heaven's sake go fix it. Don't wait around."

As some were leaving and others were getting coffee before the regular staff meeting, Jim called out, "Please sign the commitment statement. It's the same as the one you saw last week."

WEEK 12

■ Preparing for the kickoff

Carl woke up very early Tuesday morning and went right to the desk in his study to outline his talk for the kickoff. He decided that the thrust of his remarks had to be more to the problem-solving side of Continuous Improvement, rather than the management side. He'd start by reading the commitment statement, and then he'd go over the four principles, one at a time. After that, he'd tell everyone how the problem solving would take place.

His audience would mostly be interested in knowing exactly what was going to happen to them, so he'd need to describe the two workshops and the duties of the CFTs and first-level CITs when solving problems. The trick was going to be squeezing all that into thirty minutes or less.

Two days later, he opened the executive CIT meeting with a firm reminder. "If we are going to start Continuous Improvement with competence and enthusiasm, next week's kickoff meeting must be done well. I want each and every one of you to prepare your three-minute remarks carefully. We also need to be prepared to answer any and all questions about Continuous Improvement that might come up in the question-and-answer period.

"While I was preparing my talk, I started thinking about some of the kinds of questions we might be asked. Here are some I jotted down: Will my job change? How much will my job change? Is this hard work? How much time will we spend on this? Does this mean overtime? Do we do this on company time? Where will we meet? Could I lose my job? What's the training like? What do I have to do differently? Will this help me get promoted? Will we get paid more? What did the surveys say?

"Those are just a few that I came up with, and there are bound to be more. The important thing is that we don't stumble over the answers. So, what I'd like to do for the next half hour or so is practice. I'll ask a question, and you do your best to answer it."

He'd obviously caught them off guard, which was good. At the same time, he was quite pleased with most of their responses. A few of them even threw in questions of their own. Most important, he thought, they would come to the kickoff a little better prepared.

When they were done, Jim showed them the format of the new Continuous Improvement newsletter, which would be distributed at the kickoff meeting. Then Mary Louise passed out a sheet with the names and departments of all the trainer candidates she had received so far. For the balance of the hour, they discussed the various candidates and made sure all sections of the company were represented.

When they were finished, Carl closed the meeting with a reminder. "I'll see you all at the kickoff next week. Afterward, we'll meet briefly at our regular time for twenty minutes or so to make the final selection of the trainers."

MONTH 4

- **The kickoff**

- **Plans through month 8**

- **Bill's report on suppliers**

- **Jim's report on competitors**

- **Ferg's report on the surveys of internal problems and people's opinions**

Everyone got time off from work for the big kickoff meeting at the movie theater downtown. The local high-school band was pounding out the tunes of John Philip Sousa as people poured into the lobby, devoured coffee and donuts, and read copies of the new Continuous Improvement newsletter that had been left by the door. Two very large posters of Clear Run's commitment statement, with its nine signatures, were hanging on either side of the lobby next to two equally large posters stating the four principles.

At 10:00 everyone was ushered into the auditorium, where Carl and his staff were seated on the stage. After everyone settled down, Carl stepped up to the podium.

"I want to thank you all for coming," he began. "We're here because it is time—perhaps way past time—to correct some of the operational problems that have been plaguing us at Clear Run and to grab some of the operational opportunities awaiting us. You know these problems very well; you've been telling us about them for years. Well, I'm here to tell you today that we are now ready to listen.

"Most of you participated in the survey we conducted. You told us there is too much wasted time, too much bureaucracy, and too many unhappy customers because of late deliveries. There are reschedules that are very disrupting, departments and units that don't work well together, and way too much rework on products as well as on paperwork.

"At the same time, you told us about opportunities that are there for the taking—opportunities such as doing things in a way that would cut arguments and frustration, getting other departments to do their jobs right so your jobs will be easier, pleasing customers by answering and returning telephone calls, and getting departments to work together better." As the people in the audience began to recognize their input, their attention changed from merely being polite to being sincere.

"Furthermore," Carl continued, "we found that 26 percent of *all* our time was wasted doing unnecessary work, rework, follow-up, inspections and reinspections, work on poorly designed processes, and in poorly conducted meetings.

"Who's fault is this? It doesn't really matter, except that the root cause falls far more on the people sitting on this platform today, and with me, than it does on any of you.

"If we fix the problems and achieve the opportunities you've pointed out to us, we will have fewer defects, do things faster, save money, and have happier customers—which will lead to more sales. At the same time, we should *all* feel better about ourselves. There will be fewer frustrations and fewer arguments.

"To do all this, we are embarking upon a Continuous Improvement effort. As many of you know, for the last twelve weeks those of us sitting before you today have been learning about Continuous Improvement and how it will apply to the company as a whole.

"I want to do Continuous Improvement because I believe it will benefit Clear Run in three specific ways. It will help us solve operational problems and achieve operational opportunities. It will let us turn the sunshine on ourselves as our confidence soars, as our work grows more interesting, and as we each go as far as our abilities and desires will take us. And it will pave the way for us to take advantage of a whole array of advanced techniques that can help us become a superb company.

"You and the people you see sitting here with me today will all be a part of making this happen. Let me introduce them."

It was going well. The audience was interested, and they listened carefully as Carl introduced each member of the top-level CIT to explain how Continuous Improvement would benefit each department of the company. He was pleased to see they had done their homework. When they were finished, Carl returned to the podium.

"Our major goal here at Clear Run is to grow in sales and profits, and the primary way we are going to achieve this goal is through new products. Continuous Improvement will help us do that.

"I hope you read the Clear Run commitment statement that was hanging in the lobby. It has been signed by everyone you see sitting on this stage today. In case you missed it, let me read it to you now.

"We, the management of the Clear Run Company, are committed to lead in Continuous Improvement.

"We will strive to more than satisfy our customers by continuously improving our work-flow processes with help from everyone. We'll deliver on time, every time, to the agreed-upon requirements.

"In addition, we have also adopted the four principles you should have discussed in your weekly meetings and have just seen posted in the lobby. *Think work flow. Improve daily and relentlessly. Delight your customers and clients. Do things faster.* Now, principles don't mean much unless they're put into practice. Here's how we're going to do that.

"*Think work flow* first and foremost, because basic Continuous Improvement is concerned primarily with operational problems, and the root of operational problems will always be found somewhere in the flow of work—whether it's the instructions you receive, the materials you have on hand, the tools you're given to work with, or the training you've had. Work moves from person to person to person. All of us have to start thinking about the work flow in which we are involved.

"Next on the list: *Improve daily and relentlessly.* This applies to everyone. Continuous Improvement is now required of every single person who works for this organization. Each one of us is responsible every day, day after day after day, to continuously improve the work we do. To help us accomplish this, every single person in this room will attend, on company time, two workshops in which we will learn specifically how to identify and solve problems. Then everyone will become part of a problem-solving team. Each of us will then devote about two hours a week to solving problems. Some weeks you'll do more and some weeks you'll do less, but on average, over the course of a year, I'm expecting two hours a week on company time from most everyone.

"Let me explain how the company can afford to do this. Two hours a week represents a total expenditure of 5 percent of our time. If the information from our surveys is correct, we are currently wasting 26 percent of our time. So, any savings of time over and above the 5 percent we put into the effort will put us ahead.

"If you're not in sales, you may think that the third principle doesn't apply to you, but it applies to every single person in this room. *Delight your customers and clients.* If you're thinking work flow, your customer or client is the person who receives your work, whether it's a manufactured part on the assembly line, a piece of paper, or a spoken message. The major focus of most problem-solving teams will be to delight their customers, and if all your internal customers are delighted, it follows that all of our external customers will be delighted as well.

"The last principle should become your mantra. *Do things faster.* If we can make products faster, ship products faster, answer questions sooner, make decisions more quickly, beat all our competitors to market, and get financial results sooner, we will be the winners. Time is of the essence in all things. Be on the lookout, always, for ways to save it."

Harvey was standing at the back of the auditorium, his arms folded across his chest. His attention was split between Carl and the audience and how they were reacting. So far, so good.

Then Carl launched into a description of the various CITs and the first workshop and the need for trainers. When he was finished, he still had their attention.

"There is one more thing I want to say before we open the meeting to questions. All of us, from time to time, have had dreams of something the future might bring. A new car. A new house. More income. More happiness. A better job. A better life for our children.

"Another word for dreams is *vision.* The executive CIT has created a vision of what Clear Run will be like in two to three years if a substantial number of our problems are fixed and many opportunities are realized. I'd like to read it to you now.

"In two to three years, Clear Run will be the supplier of first choice for 95 percent of its customers.

"Most of our people will run—not walk—to work because they enjoy what they do, because it's a pleasure for them to deal with their peers, and because they all feel they have helped themselves improve.

"Everyone will spend some time, daily and relentlessly, on improving what he or she does.

"And most of the waste will have been designed out of the work, work will be done faster, schedules and promises will always be met, and everyone will be working on opportunities.

"As you embark on Continuous Improvement with us, I want each of you to form your own vision. Focus on what your own job will be like and how you will feel once all the problems that now plague you are solved and all the opportunities you've had to ignore can be achieved.

"It's out there for all of us, but it will take hard work and persistence. There are no shortcuts, no magic potions, and no miracles.

"My job is to lead us through Continuous Improvement, but I need your help, your enthusiasm, and your dedication to make it happen. We're in this together. Let's go make our vision and our dreams come true."

Carl paused and there was an unexpected round of applause from the audience. A few people were still staring skeptically, but for the most part everyone seemed enthused. When the clapping stopped, Carl suggested they stand and stretch for a couple of minutes. He then he opened the floor to questions.

The next day, the executive CIT met and selected thirty-five trainers. Mary Louise reminded them once again that when all was said and done, they would probably only end up with twenty-five, including herself, but that would be plenty.

After the meeting, Ferg buttonholed Carl and they walked back to Carl's office together. "What's gotten into you?" asked Ferg.

"What do you mean?"

"You're getting all warm and cuddly. You're acting as if you really like people again. The old Carl just pounded the table and set goals and didn't listen. What happened?"

"Maybe I'm just getting smarter as I grow up," said Carl. "Let me tell you a little story. Some time ago, when I was just starting out, my boss did something that really angered me. Being the new kid on the block, I had no recourse, so instead I jotted down how I wanted to be treated. I wanted to be treated with respect; listened to, not yelled at; given a task to do and left alone to do it; challenged to do more than currently expected; not be checked-up on all the time; trusted to be responsible; treated as an individual; and to have my brain used. I started thinking about that list a few weeks ago when I started thinking about how I would get everyone in the organization as enthused about Continuous Improvement as I am.

"Once processes start being improved," Carl continued, "and the organization is wasting less time, people will no longer be looked upon as cogs in a wheel, doing what they have been told to do. Not only that, management will have the time to turn their attention to each individual's concerns, needs, and aspirations. It will all happen from a humanistic point of view and will, coincidentally, benefit the entire organization. So, if I'm going to lead us through Continuous Improvement, I guess I better lead in this area as well."

Ferg laughed and patted Carl on the back. "Welcome," he said. "We're glad you're back."

By the following week, everyone on the executive CIT had received some positive feedback from the big kickoff. The air was charged with excitement, but Harvey felt compelled to bring them back to earth.

"That was a great meeting. I was proud of all of you. But I would not be doing my job if I didn't warn you that there will be resistance. You will probably see it as soon as people start thinking up excuses to miss the first training session."

"Harvey, do me a favor," said Carl. "Allow me to feel good right now."

"Sorry. Just consider yourselves warned."

"Well, the comments of Dr. Doom aside, let's talk a bit about what we'll be doing in the following months. There are eight parts left from our original list of fifteen, six of which must be done right away. We still need to finish collecting problems and opportunities and training everyone. Then we need to select five top-priority problems or opportunities, express the five as goals, hold everyone accountable, and appreciate and reward achievement. The last two, modify prior operating guidelines and transition Continuous Improvement into the ongoing management of the organization, come much later. What I'd like to do from now on is to make each of these items our main focus for each of the coming months.

"The first part of each meeting will focus on the topic for the month. Then, in the last fifteen or twenty minutes, we can talk about the ongoing effort. So, with that in mind, we need to focus on collecting problems and opportunities again."

There was a collective groan from everyone in the room. "I warned you," said Harvey. "The resistance has already begun."

"Listen," said Carl. "We have to do this. Part ten, select five top-priority problems or opportunities, must be finished. If we don't take the time to explore every nook and cranny for problems to solve, what kind of example are we setting for everyone else?"

He turned to Bill. "Are you ready with your supplier survey?"

"As most of you know," said Bill, "we have problems getting materials to specifications. We reject over 3 percent of what we receive. However, last year our material review board *accepted* 135 lots of material that were not to specification—either the deviation was not critical or we changed our processes to use the faulty material. Therefore, a real candidate for improvement here is to get our suppliers to ship us only material that meets the specs so that our material review board can be completely disbanded. Thirty vendors supply more than 98 percent of the materials we use to make our products; that's 98 percent in terms of dollars spent. In order to get all of them to respond to the survey, I had our purchasing agent hand each supplier's salesperson or manager the survey and go over it with him or her face to face. The good news is that all thirty responded. The bad news is that we are not sure their answers were completely candid.

"In any case, the survey pointed out that sometimes suppliers were shipping to *their* specifications, not ours. Some of them felt we were arbitrary on issues; others felt we were capricious. One said, 'I didn't take your specifications seriously when the drawings arrived with coffee stains on them.' And most felt our frequent order changes put a rush on certain materials, causing poor quality.

"We have mailed the survey to the rest of our suppliers, the ones who provide equipment, spare parts, machinery, printing, supplies, and so forth. We haven't gotten all those back yet. I'd like to give them another week or two."

Jim was next. "I don't think I have anything new to say about our competitors that you haven't already heard. Nor have I made a formal gathering of facts, but I *can* sum up where we stand in general.

"In regard to meeting what customers want on current purchase orders—and that means on-time delivery and no errors in products or paperwork—we are equal to our U.S. competitors, somewhat behind our Japanese competitors, and somewhat ahead of our European competitors. However, none of us comes even close to what the customers really want.

"So, all we need to do for the next few years on our current product line is to meet what the customers want, and we won't even have to worry about the competition.

"In the field of new products," Jim continued, "we are behind our competitors in moving our ideas from conception to production. We have good ideas. We're as good as anybody in the world on ideas. But we fall down on execution. Again, there is no sense in making a detailed comparison to our competitors. We've simply got to go faster."

"It sounds as if a formal comparison to competitors is not even needed," said Elaine.

"No, it's just not needed now. But once we get really hot, the comparison may very well be needed to find out how we can be even better."

As Cam and Carol had nothing to add to the reports they had given earlier on quality performance and customers, Carl turned the meeting over to a general discussion on what was going on.

Mary Louise reported that she had held the first meeting with the trainers, had given each of them a training manual to read, and had scheduled the first part of their training.

Elaine announced that people in finance and accounting were strongly in favor of the effort. "The three people in accounts receivable have already found some ways to reduce the amount of money owed to us."

Cam, however, complained that things were moving too slowly. "Is there anything we can do to pick up the pace?" he asked.

"I feel the same way," said Carl. "That's why I told you all last week to go solve some problems *now*. But for the time being we need to stick to the schedule. We need to train the trainers and have them practice before the actual training workshops begin. That will take at least six weeks. If you're itchy to start—and I hope you are—we should see a great demand for training on the front end of the schedule. Once 50 percent of the members of a first-level CIT have gone through the first workshop, I see no reason why they all—the trained and the yet to be trained—couldn't officially start their problem solving.

"Anyway, over the next two weeks we will finish up the part on collecting problems and opportunities with Ferg's results of the internal survey and pay some special attention to certain kinds of problems."

Ferg was ready the following week.

"As you remember, I was commissioned to run a survey," said Ferg, holding up copies of the Internal Survey of Problems and the Survey of People's Opinions. "Seventy-nine percent of the people in the company participated, and at least 45 percent of the people in each department filled one out. By the way, I want to thank all of you for helping to get your people to the cafeteria when scheduled. A little over half of the surveys were signed. And remember, these surveys were filled out by supervisors and managers as well." Ferg had seven piles of paper, one for each manager in attendance, which he proceeded to distribute.

"The Survey of People's Opinions, in particular, has given us a lot of good information and will provide a baseline for comparison when we run the survey again twelve months from now.

"Now, there are all kinds of fancy things we can do with the numbers," he said. "But, for the time being, I suggest that each of you read the material I'm passing you now, which is basically just raw data, and summarize what is pertinent to your department. I've already looked it over and didn't see any great surprises. Most of the ratings on the Survey of People's Opinions were from 3.0 to 4.0, which means that they agreed or agreed positively with the various statements. What I would like you to pay special attention to, however, are the discordant ratings or the discordant problems—things we have totally overlooked or issues about which people are really unhappy.

"Next month, when we start deciding which problems or opportunities to work on, you'll have even more data. That way, when your departments start selecting problems to work on, they will have a head start."

The team members dug into the information, and a lively discussion followed for the rest of the meeting and well into the next one.

By the time they were done, Elaine had just one question. "You've all been thinking 'problems and opportunities' for the last sixteen weeks. When do we start thinking 'work flow'?"

"The principle 'think work flow,'" explained Ferg, "leads people to understand that somewhere in their work flow they will find the causes of *operational* problems and their solutions. So, in a roundabout way, we actually *are* getting at work flow. We just have to be careful not to overlook our *major* and *critical* work-flow processes."

Elaine was still confused.

"Major work flows—and it's possible we don't have more than ten—are the major arteries of the company," explained Ferg. "They include such things as the order-through-manufacturing flow and the accounting system. Critical work flows are usually short, but are just as vital to our existence. They include such things as setting prices and hiring people. If any of these work flows are not operating optimally, they need to be added to our list of problems. I'm glad you brought it up, Elaine."

Seeing there were no more questions, Ferg wrapped things up. "I must say, I've been here for more than twenty years and we've never collected information like this before. It was about time."

The discussion turned to other issues. Mary Louise reported that the trainers had just gone through Workshop 1 and had already started to practice teaching it. Three of the trainers had dropped out already for various reasons, but the rest were still enthusiastic.

"Are there any issues coming back up the ladder that we should know about or discuss?" asked Carl. There were none. "Well," he persisted, "is anything going down the ladder? Are you and your people holding your weekly meetings? I had a 'Coffee with Carl' session earlier this week and only three-fourths of the people there had been to a meeting in the past month. That's not good enough."

"Well," said Bill, "we've been trying, but it's not easy when I haven't yet provided adequate meeting space, especially for the first-level CITs."

"Please hold the meetings," Carl insisted. "They are critical to getting people prepared to start something new."

MONTH 5

- **Selecting five top-priority problems or opportunities**

- **More on training**

"Our task this month," said Carl, patting a huge pile of paper in front of him, "is to boil this stack of problems and opportunities down to five top-priority problems or opportunities. These will be the top five for the company. Each one will be solved in one of two ways. It will either go to a CFT selected by us with one of you as the sponsor, or it will be assigned directly to one of you, who will solve the problem in your department and units as you see fit. We, as a team, won't actually solve problems. We will, however, manage or oversee the problem-solving teams."

"What do you mean by manage or oversee the problem-solving teams?" asked Carol.

"Well, we will personally review the five problem-solving teams we're responsible for and make sure they're working toward their goals. If any get off track, it's our job to take corrective action and get them back on track."

"Why five?" asked Moe.

"Five just seems like a manageable number for us as a team. Fewer would be too unambitious, and any more would tend to dilute our attention.

"Now, the mid-level CITs—and we have fifteen of them—will manage three problems or opportunities at any one time. They, too, will appoint CFTs or assign the responsibility to the first-level CITs in their department.

"The first-level CITs—we have sixty of them—will each solve one, maybe two, problems at a time in their problem-solving meetings.

"If each first-level team is working on one problem, each mid-level team is overseeing three, and we are responsible for five, then Clear Run should be working on 110 problems at any one time. That's quite a handful. However, there will be occasions when more than one CIT will be responsible for the same problem. For example, if Bill's mid-level CIT has responsibility for one of the five problems that we're overseeing, that team would select only two of its own."

"Are we supposed to select problems for the mid- and first-level CITs as well?" asked Elaine.

"Not necessarily, but we can if we think it is necessary. Basically, they should select their own problems to work on using the data we collected and problems and opportunities they identify on their own.

"What we need to do today," Carl continued, "is to go through this pile in front of me and narrow it down to twenty problems. In two weeks we will narrow that list down to five.

"There are a few things we need to keep in mind as we do this. First of all, we can't take on abstract problems such as 'low morale' without first identifying what might be contributing to low morale, things such as impossible work assignments, weak supervisors, or unpleasant physical work areas—things we *can* solve.

"We might also need to narrow down some very broad problems. Let's say we want high ratings from all of our customers. We could start by choosing ten customers and getting high ratings from them. Or suppose we want to improve the quality of all the products we manufacture. We could select only three or four product lines as a start. In short, we need to refine broad and fuzzy problems into concrete and narrow problems."

"Shouldn't we try to refine some now to get an idea of how it is done?" asked Ferg.

"This will be covered in Workshop 1," answered Carl, "but let's try one now anyway. How about poor communications?" he said, striding to the chart pad. "That's a fuzzy one."

"Poor communications between the plants and the new products people," offered Bill.

"Between which two groups?" asked Carl.

"Well, between the designers and purchasing."

"Which part of each?"

"Between the designers of major new products and the material buyers."

"What specifically is the problem?" asked Carl.

"Well, the major new product designers continue to select coatings from suppliers who are incapable of meeting specifications, quality levels, or delivery schedules, so the material buyers are not placing the orders."

"Now we're getting somewhere," said Carl as he drew a line through "poor communications" and restated the problem as Bill had just described it.

"I get it," said Bill. "*That* is something we can solve."

"Right. Now I'd like each of you to write, on a sheet of chart paper, five somewhat narrowly defined problems or opportunities that will still be of sufficient magnitude to be of interest to this group. When you're done, hang your sheet on the wall and we'll start the process of combining similar problems and eliminating duplicates until we narrow them down to twenty or less. You've got fifteen minutes."

Narrowing the fifty down to twenty-five didn't pose much of a problem, but some serious arguments erupted when they began whittling away at the twenty-five. In the end, they agreed on sixteen:

- Complete the order-to-shipment tracking system
- Meet the deadline for the engine-control project
- Reduce people turnover
- Reduce customer credits for all nonproduct reasons
- Reduce purchases of defective material
- Increase teamwork
- Improve communications
- Eliminate the bureaucracy and red tape and those practices, policies, and procedures that hinder progress
- Reduce the number of defective parts shipped to customers
- Please the top ten customers
- Improve maintenance of manufacturing equipment
- Produce the major new product on time
- Improve training
- Make better choices on investments in plant and equipment
- Streamline the budgeting process
- Eliminate poor meetings

"That's a good start," said Carl. "Over the next week, you can all think about how we might pare this down even more. Remember, we want only five."

During the next week, Carl attended one of the trainers' practice sessions. He was more than a little impressed. The trainers came from all levels and parts of the organization, yet they all treated each other with respect and courtesy. They were all excited about the future, particularly the prospect of helping people solve the problems in their own work.

"This is a very inclusive activity," one of the trainers said to Carl. "I'm impressed. Everyone in the company will take the same course. We'll all be treated alike, and we will all treat each other alike as well."

At the next executive CIT meeting, Mary Louise announced that they were just about ready to launch the training, big time. There would be two practice workshops the following week, so they could test the material and teaching techniques before going full-steam ahead. Everyone on the executive CIT was invited to attend, either as a participant or an observer.

"This could give some of you a head start," Carl reminded them.

"I must have missed something," said Carol. "What exactly are we going to learn at the workshops?"

"Perhaps we didn't cover it," said Mary Louise, "with all that has been going on. Workshop 1, which takes nine hours, involves the participants in solving a problem from the Surfside Market Case, a short case included in the manual. The manual also includes twenty-two problem-solving techniques. The participants, broken into small teams, all solve the same problem using most of those techniques. The trainers simply guide the participants through the process.

"Workshop 2, Pete's Puppy Pen Case, is six hours long and should be held about eight weeks later. In it, the participants use the balance of the techniques in the manual by learning how to chart a process and then improve it."

Mary Louise passed out the schedule with a list of workshop locations. "We've decided that Workshop 1 should be taught on two consecutive days of four and one-half hours each," she said. "I'll have this list posted by tomorrow and start taking sign-ups then."

Carl was afraid some of them weren't paying attention. "Let there be no ambiguity, misunderstanding, confusion, or hearing impairment," he said. "Everyone—including all of you and me—has two months in which to get trained. It is a requirement for everyone—no ifs, ands, or buts."

By the next meeting the sixteen problems and opportunities identified two weeks before had been legibly rewritten on four sheets of chart paper. The task today was to narrow it down to five.

"Do we have any criteria?" asked Moe. "The five easiest? The five toughest? Or just those that will benefit customers? I think we should have criteria before we start."

"Let's just pick 'em," said Bill. "I'm tired of selecting problems and opportunities. We've been at this now for five months. Let's get off the pot!"

"Yeah," said Cam. "It's not critical that we pick the perfect five. After all, we're going to be at this forever."

It looked like they were going nowhere fast, and Carl wasn't sure how to focus them. Fortunately, Harvey stepped into the ring. "Can I say something?" he asked. "Looking at some of the data you've collected, talking to various people, and thinking about other projects I have worked on at Clear Run, I think it's clear that *most* of the problems you have throughout the company revolve around poor teamwork and poor communications, which almost always comes down to a lack of understanding between units over what is to be done, by whom, and when.

"I think you would solve a lot of problems in one swoop if your first-level CITs focused on establishing clear requirements for the work to be done between themselves and their customers and suppliers. Then you should ban the words *teamwork* and *communications* and force people to do what Carl and Bill did two weeks ago when they boiled 'poor communications' down to a specific issue between the design engineers and the material buyers."

Moe in particular thought this was a good idea, and he promised to pass it down through the ranks in his department.

Ferg asked to move the item on bureaucracy, red tape, practices, policies, and procedures to the bottom of the list, but only because it would require some special consideration. "There is a lot there that needs to be corrected," he confirmed.

Jim and Carol together pleaded that the group select those items that would have the quickest and greatest impact on customers—leading to more sales and more profit—as the top five. No one disagreed, but Carl was concerned. "If that leads us to five that are very encompassing and difficult to attain, it might be too much at one time. We need, perhaps, to have one or two that will guarantee success."

"Let's just pick 'em," said Bill again.

"Okay," said Carol. "I'll start. Complete the order-to-shipment tracking system, meet the deadline for the engine-control project, and reduce defective parts shipped."

Carl wrote them down on a new sheet of chart paper, and then noticed that Moe was looking anxious.

"Is there something you want to add?" Carl asked.

"I want the major new product on the list. It's our future. It's a necessity. My department needs to do a better job, and I need all the help I can beg, borrow, and steal from the rest of you."

Carl added "produce the major new product on time" to the list.

There was one more to select. A lot of discussion ensued, but Carl didn't write anything down. In the parlance of trainers, he was goal tending—he didn't write until he agreed with the speaker.

"I suggest we include 'reduce customer credits for administrative reasons,'" said Carol. "They are all paperwork errors, and it's a perfect example of the kind of thing that plagues the sales department and our customers. On top of that, it should be pretty easy to fix." Nobody argued, so Carl added it as the fifth choice.

"Our next big job will be to turn these five problems and opportunities into goal statements," he said. "We'll start working on that next week, but in the meantime we need to select a sponsor for each of these, one of us who will oversee each project and report back to us. Ferg, you've already got the order-to-shipment tracking system and a CFT working on it, so that's easy. And likewise for Bill with the engine-control project. Now, who should sponsor 'reduce defective parts shipped'?"

"Perhaps Cam and I should handle it together," said Bill. "We can manage this through my mid-level CIT, though Cam would be doing the bulk of the work."

"Let's stick to one name."

"Okay. Let's make it Cam."

"The major new product should be mine," said Moe.

"That leaves 'reduce customer administrative credits,'" said Carl. "Do I have any takers?"

"That one touches a lot of departments," said Elaine. "Sales, product engineering, shipping, and accounting. Carol and Bill are already plenty busy, and we should save Jim for a biggie. So I'll take it and form a CFT to solve the problem."

When they were done, Carl stood back from the chart paper and revealed the list.

Opportunity	Sponsor	Team
Order-to-shipment tracking system	Ferg	CFT
Engine-control project	Bill	CFT
Reduce defective parts shipped	Cam	Mid-level CIT
Major new product	Moe	Mid-level CIT
Reduce administrative credits	Elaine	CFT

"Okay," said Carl. "How about your mid-level CITs? Any progress yet in selecting *their* three problems?"

"Well," said Bill, "the engine-control project is well under way, so we won't count that, but we will count the reduction of defective parts. That leaves two, and believe me, we have a long list of candidates."

"I know you want three," said Moe, "but I want every living, breathing moment of all my people focused on completing this one project on time."

"Done," said Carl. "I agree with you 100 percent. One it is."

"The sales department is so perfect," said Carol, "that finding even one skimpy little problem to work on will be a major task."

"What have you been smoking?" asked Bill.

"Just joking. We'll find and fix three. And you can bet money we'll fix them well."

Elaine had a question. "As I understand it, each first-level CIT will just identify one or two problems and then just fix them, right? Our only obligation, as far as they're concerned, is to offer guidance only if there's something in particular we feel is important."

"Right," said Carl, "and don't start thinking that just because you're not a sponsor you won't have anything to do. Each and every one of you, and everyone on a mid-level CIT, is a candidate for one of the CFTs. We've got three here already," he said, pointing to his list, "and who knows how many the mid-level CITs will come up with. You will all have an opportunity to participate—with love and joy in your hearts."

In the few minutes remaining, Mary Louise gave her report on training progress. "The two workshop dress rehearsals went well. I'm pleased that three of you participated, and I presume we'll see the rest of you in class over the next eight weeks. We now have twenty-five competent trainers suited up and ready to trot out onto the field. The posted schedules are filling up—but slowly. We still have plenty of space open in the first few weeks. So," she pleaded, "get after your people to sign up."

MONTH 6

- **Setting the five top-priority goals**
- **More on training**
- **Establishing guidelines for first-level CIT problem-solving meetings**

The next order of business was to convert the five problems the executive CIT had agreed upon into five goals. Harvey was very good at this sort of thing, so Carl asked him to give his team some ideas. Harvey began with an acronym that, he hoped, everyone would remember: SMART.

"Goals must be SMART," he said. "Specific. Measurable. Agreed upon. Realistic. Timed. They must be *specifically* defined so you know what you're doing; *measurable* because if you don't measure it, you'll find that it won't get fixed; *agreed upon* between the people doing the work and their customer or supplier or between the team and its manager or supervisor; *realistic* in light of the difficulty, the time, and the resources being applied; and finally, *timed,* meaning each has a start date and a finish date.

"Having said that, I should add that goals don't have to have a quantifiable outcome. In some cases, you may simply document the process change made. For example, an administrative assistant solves the problem of not being able to easily find papers and documents by going to a new filing system. The stated goal would simply be to change to a new filing system by a certain date. Or, if you're dealing with a wretched mailing list because it's out of date, just set a goal of installing a new mailing list method by a certain date.

"Also," he continued, "don't hold people and teams to the standard that a goal can never be missed. You want people to set challenging goals—to reach out and be imaginative. Good progress *toward* meeting a challenging goal, even if it isn't attained, should be appreciated and rewarded as much as meeting a less challenging goal."

Seeing that Harvey was finished, Carl flipped the chart paper to the list of their five goals.

"Okay," said Carl, "let's just go right down the list. Ferg, why don't you start by turning the order-to-shipment tracking system into a goal?"

Ferg cleared his throat and began. "The order-to-shipment tracking system is an unusual, all-encompassing effort to improve our logistics. It encompasses the totality of logistics from the time the customer raises his hand and says 'I am here' until..."

"Ferg," Carl interrupted, "what's the goal?"

"...until the customer receives and pays us for the product. Each step in the process has a series of tests to see that a function is on schedule."

"Ferg, what's the goal?"

"Well," said Ferg, "there are many goals, but they're really too arcane to be explained briefly to a group like this."

"Let me try," said Carol. "The goal of the order-to-shipment tracking system is to design a method that will allow us to deliver products by the promised delivery date 100 percent of the time. If it doesn't do that, it's a bust."

"Right," said Carl, "that's the idea. Now we just need to assign a date for when this performance will be met."

"Wait a minute," said Jim. "We can measure on-time delivery with a number, but how do we measure whether customers are satisfied?"

"You could use the Customer or Client Survey," said Harvey. "The data come back as numbers and is called a satisfaction index. You can even track progress over time by taking subsequent surveys."

Once Carl was convinced everyone understood the process, he asked Ferg, Bill, Cam, Moe, and Elaine to prepare a SMART goal for each of their respective problems by the following week. He then asked Mary Louise to report on training, which had just begun in earnest.

"So far, so good," she said. "I am, however, getting concerned by the lack of meeting space available to the problem-solving teams, which are nearly ready to go. I would like to get together with Ferg and Bill after this meeting and talk about where we might find some space and the necessary tables, chairs, and easels, and what it might cost.

"And there's another thing," she added. "The training schedule for Workshop 1 is lightly filled for the first few weeks, and then it starts getting packed and is sold out in the last two weeks. Please try to move some people into those first weeks so we don't have such a logjam at the end and so people can start solving problems sooner. Also, we're going to need some space during the last sessions for makeups, so the earlier we get people scheduled, the better."

Ferg gave the problem of setting a goal for the order-to-shipment tracking system to the reengineering task force, which was now called a CFT. Using paper and computers, the new system would cover everything from order inquiry through shipment, billing, and collecting. Raw material purchases, product movement through the plants, and inventory status would also be covered. The idea was to completely revamp the old system, which had grown hit or miss from the company's inception and was probably responsible for Clear Run's record of missing promised delivery dates 33 percent of the time. The reengineering task force had been working on the new system for twelve months. Within a week, however, Ferg had coaxed a concrete goal out of them to report back to the executive CIT.

"The new order-to-shipment tracking system will reduce the number of missed promise dates for all orders to 5 percent by Continuous Improvement calendar month 23," he announced. "The team wanted me to negotiate an escape clause, but I said no dice."

"What do you mean by an escape clause?" asked Jim.

"They wanted it contingent upon people using the new process properly, for one thing," Ferg replied. "I told them we were not going to have any goals with loopholes and neither was anybody else in the company."

"I agree wholeheartedly," said Carl.

When it was Bill's turn to announce the goal for the engine-control project, he invited Teresa, the new project leader, to lead the discussion. She brought the entire CFT to help her put on a first-class dog and pony show, which they had perfected over the last fifteen months by making presentations to their customer.

"As most of you know," she began, "this is a huge project for Clear Run. This product goes to one automotive customer as part of a new engine-control mechanism, but in terms of dollar volume, we are selling more of this single part than any other part in the company."

Teresa and her team then showed slides of Clear Run inside and out, gave a history of the company, described the product, and launched into a discussion describing how they planned to improve the defect level from 100 to 10 ppm. "We've spent a great deal of time with the customer agreeing on the testing methods and equipment," she said. "Then we purchased test equipment that was exactly the same as the customer's test equipment so we'd be comparing apples with apples.

"The Concord plant, where this part is made, has put in some special equipment for this part, and all the process steps are precisely monitored. Stress testing revealed some weaknesses in the design, which were rectified by a new design and some new processing steps. We are currently shipping at 100 ppm defective—down from 1,000 ppm at the project's start—and are confident that the new design changes will take us to 10 ppm by month 12. That's our goal."

"What will the customer do if we can't meet 10 ppm?" asked Jim. "Will they take their business elsewhere? Do we have a backup plan?"

"No, we don't need one," said Teresa. "We know we'll be at 10 ppm because our processes are under control."

Cam was next. "As far as the number of defective parts shipped goes," said Cam, "we are currently at 3,000 ppm for all products. Our goal is to ship fewer than 300 ppm defective by month 18.

"Let me amplify this a bit," he added. "The 300-ppm goal is just an average. We will have many products under 100 ppm, but we will also have some problem children that will take quite a bit of work to get down to 300 ppm, including new products, some of the specials we make for certain customers, and parts we receive from our sister companies and sell to our customers."

"What are the customers' requirements?" asked Carl.

"They average around 1,000 ppm, but we expect them to lower them to 300 ppm at about the same time we are shipping at 300 ppm."

"This goal is very doable," added Bill, "because we have the engine-control project as a model. What we learned on that we are now applying to all products and processes. And we have a not-so-secret weapon. A year ago we added Jeff, a statistician who is an expert in the statistical design of experiments, to our team. He has already had a strong impact on improved yield and defect reduction."

When Cam and Bill were finished, Moe took the floor.

"Our goal for the major new product," he said, "is to have ten thousand pieces in inventory by month 18 and to issue a press release at that time announcing that the product is available for sale. Then, about four months after the product is released, we'll do a customer satisfaction survey to get an accurate assessment of the product's future. Our goal is to have 25 percent of the ranking at 5.0, 50 percent at 4.0, 25 percent at 3.0, and nothing below that."

Elaine had pulled together a CFT of five people to work on reducing customer administrative credits. They were there to back her up when it was her turn to announce their goal. "We are still in the exploration stage," she admitted, "but we do know these credits have been running at 1.5 percent of sales for a long time. According to the preliminary data we've collected, it looks like half of the problem lies in the sales department. It turns out that Clear Run's paperwork after entering the order does not match the customer's order paperwork."

Everyone looked at Carol, who was holding her hands over her face. "Elaine told me yesterday," she admitted. "This is very embarrassing, particularly since I've been blaming everyone else."

"Well, don't feel bad," said Elaine, "you're not alone. There are also shipping errors, packing errors, and billing errors. Given the fact that Carol will probably pull her group together on this, we think a goal of 0.3 percent customer administrative credits by month 18 is fairly realistic."

"That's a fivefold improvement in just twelve months," said Jim. "Are you sure you can do it?"

"Well, we might be nuts, but up until now the only thing we've ever done about this problem is bitch about it. Now we know how to improve it. So we're going to stick with 0.3 percent."

"Good," said Carl, who was putting the finishing touches on a chart he'd been working on at the easel (see p. 100). "Here's where we stand on our top five goals." He read from the easel, going down the list one by one, identifying the opportunity, the goal, the sponsor, and the team.

"I hope you're all as pleased as I am with this list," said Carl. "If the engine-control project meets its goal, we'll start seeing some significant changes around here in as little as six months. That's phenomenal. Next month we'll establish a method for holding everyone accountable for results to make sure we get problems solved and opportunities achieved.

"Meanwhile, I've asked Jim to tell us a little about what his team is up to and to give us some ideas about implementation that we can all use."

Jim stepped to the chart paper and revealed a drawing of his organizational chart (see p. 101). "The top triangle is my mid-level CIT," Jim explained. "The members, with the exception of my administrative assistant, who is represented by the circle that stands alone and who is not a CIT member, each supervise one of six first-level CITs. The numbers indicate the number of people in each CIT. Eighty percent of these people have been through Workshop 1—including all the supervisors and myself—so we are more than ready to start solving problems. We have been holding our weekly, mid-level, thirty-minute CIT meetings religiously. The first-level, ten-minute CIT meetings have been held about 75 percent of the time, and we are now ready to add the fifty minutes per week for problem solving.

Top Five Goals

Opportunity	Goal	Sponsor	Team
Order-to-shipment tracking system	Less than 5 percent missed shipments to the promised dates by month 23	Ferg	CFT
Engine-control project	10 ppm by month 12	Bill	CFT
Reduce defective parts shipped	Less than 300 ppm by month 18	Cam	Mid-level CIT
Major new product	Ten thousand pieces in inventory by month 18 with a press release announcing the product for sale; survey of customer satisfaction four months later with 25 percent at 5.0, 50 percent at 4.0, and 25 percent at 3.0	Moe	Mid-level CIT
Reduce administrative credits	0.3 percent errors by month 18	Elaine	CFT

"As an aside," said Jim, "people were told before the training that we would be meeting for one hour a week, but that we would also be required to spend another hour on problem solving outside the meeting. Now, from Workshop 1, they understand that outside the meeting they will be gathering data, seeing customers and suppliers, and planning and implementing the agreed-upon changes.

"In regard to the physical setup, I insisted that each first-level CIT meet for one hour in the same room or meeting area at the same time each week. I'm convinced that the discipline of a weekly meeting holds the key to progress. We are not requiring that they keep minutes, but we have urged them to keep notes for themselves. We also had a long discussion about attendance and decided it was up to the supervisors to be sure that everyone participated, just as they do now on any job assignment.

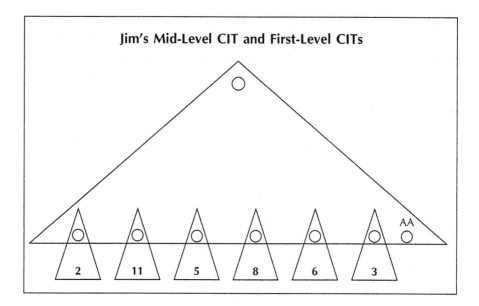

Jim's Mid-Level CIT and First-Level CITs

"We have also had people attend meetings via telephone conference calls. While it's not the best way to conduct a meeting, it does work and it's better than not having the people participate at all."

Carol was particularly interested in this last bit of news because she was still anticipating huge problems with her salespeople in the field.

"In operations, we came up with a couple of different solutions to the same kinds of problems," said Bill. "We have some jobs that are very routine, such as people loading and unloading machines. And we have some people in isolated work, such as drivers and maintenance people on the swing and night shifts. Although they are attending Workshop 1, having these people in weekly meetings for an hour really doesn't make sense. One solution is for their supervisors to talk to them and bring their ideas to a problem-solving meeting. Another is to post the problem under discussion and have them add their ideas using self-adhesive notes."

"Well done," said Carl. "Let me just add a few thoughts of my own. First of all, don't be afraid to move people around in those first-level CITs so that you get the right people working on a problem. No one should be on a team solving a problem that does not concern them. If need be, people can be loaned from one CIT to another if they have some special insight or experience that will help the other CIT.

"Another thing is that no CIT should have more than ten members. If it does, it should be broken into two CITs."

The meeting closed, as it did every week, with Mary Louise's report on training. The news this week was not very encouraging. "According to my records, only 80 percent of our people have gone through, or signed up for, Workshop 1. The last two weeks are almost completely booked. Meanwhile, we've got workshops going on right now that are begging for more participants. Please don't wait until the last minute."

MONTH 7

- **Establishing a method for holding everyone accountable for Continuous Improvement results**

- **Three ways to display progress toward goals**

- **Key results indicators**

- **More on training**

Now that the five problems had been expressed as goals, Carl's next task was to devise a way to measure everyone's progress without inspiring moans and groans from his staff for wrapping them up in more red tape. For ongoing operations, his was a management-by-objective system with lots of sales, financial, project, personal performance, and salary reviews—what amounted to a lot of unnecessary bureaucracy in the eyes of some of his staff, but what represented sound, solid management procedures to Carl.

His first inclination was to use the same procedures for Continuous Improvement. But maybe, he thought, he should start with a blank sheet of paper and try to come up with some alternatives. After crumpling a lot of paper and tossing it in the general direction of the wastebasket, he came away with two ideas that would satisfy his own needs and, he hoped, keep the troops happy. One was to get each team's accomplishments onto a single sheet of paper. The other was to limit himself to asking no more than two questions of each member of his staff to assure himself that each department was on track. Once his thoughts became somewhat clear, he called Mary Louise, Elaine, Harvey, and Ferg to his office.

"I have been wracking my brains to find a simple way to measure everyone's progress on Continuous Improvement, and I think I've finally got it," he said. "First of all, I will ask only two questions. I might ask, 'How many teams do you have in your department?' Or, 'What problems or opportunities are you working on at the current moment?'

"Then," he said, "I will ask each team to fill out a one-page results form (see p. 105) whenever it solves a problem, achieves an opportunity, or reaches a milestone."

"One page?" asked Ferg incredulously.

"One page," confirmed Carl, "Take a look." And he handed each of them a copy of the form he had worked out.

"This can be posted for peers to read, reviewed by the CI counselor, printed in the newsletter, and used as a basis for public appreciation. What do you think? Do we need anything else?"

"I think we need a way to chart results," said Elaine.

"Fine," said Carl. "Any ideas on *how*?"

"Well," she said, "we could report the actual results versus the goals in a graph or a table. Or we could simply list documented changes."

"We need some kind of review process as well," said Ferg.

"How about if each CIT's performance is reviewed by the next highest level of supervision?" said Harvey. "CFTs could be reviewed by their sponsor and the sponsoring CIT. The results form could provide a pretty good basis for these reviews. The more results forms a team hands in, the better the performance."

These were all good ideas, but the best part was that Carl couldn't be accused of complicating the issue when he broached the subject at the next meeting. He did, however, feel compelled to elaborate. "Let's not beat people up with these reviews," he cautioned. "The root cause of almost all operational problems can be found in the work-flow process. So, when something goes wrong, don't ask, 'Who did it?' Ask, instead, 'What is wrong with the process?' These reviews should be opportunities for learning, coaching, and helping, not for criticizing."

"Are we going to do any reviews of individual performance?" asked Mary Louise.

"Not yet," said Carl. "I want to keep the focus on the team approach at this time. But, of course, we will start to include Continuous Improvement tasks on our regular performance review forms.

"Look Ma, no hands, no red tape," said Carl, throwing his hands in the air. "Ask only two questions. Look at some charts. Hold reviews. And receive results forms. What could be simpler?"

Results

Team name: Today's date:

Leader: Starting date:

Members:

Problem or opportunity expressed as a goal:

Describe the solution (list the key processes changed, eliminated, or added):

Results:

Benefits (including, if possible, projected annual savings):

"This is too slick," said Ferg. "There must be a few cards up your sleeve!"

"No sir! By the way," Carl added, "do we even have any problem-solving teams yet?"

"Yes," said Mary Louise. "Some first-level CITs have added the fifty minutes to their meetings, so they can start identifying and solving problems. We have assigned a trainer to each of these teams to serve as a coach and to make sure everyone stays on track with the problem-solving method we all learned."

"Will every first-level CIT and CFT be assigned a coach?" asked Elaine.

"Sure," said Mary Louise. "The trainers signed on knowing we'd need coaches, and they are the best prepared to help for the time being."

"I assume everyone will be trained by the end of this month," Carl said to the group as a whole. "We will have 100 percent attendance, correct?"

Everyone nodded, but not with a great deal of conviction.

By the following week, Carl had decided on a formal schedule for progress reports. "Every six weeks the sponsor will give a ten-minute review of his or her top-priority goal," said Carl. "The review will be orchestrated by the sponsor, who either will give an updated status report and describe the future plans of the goal by himself or herself or will assign the project leader to do so.

"In between these reviews, we should hear nothing about the top five unless one of them rolls off course or there is a need for some specific help."

Cam, who had already given this some thought, offered some ideas to the group. "I can visualize this meeting room serving as our chart room," he began, "with charts detailing our progress toward our top five goals and the three goals of the mid-level CITs. After our last meeting, I went back to my office and played around a little with the various ways to do this. I came up with three different methods."

Cam put one of them on an overhead projector so everyone could see it (see below).

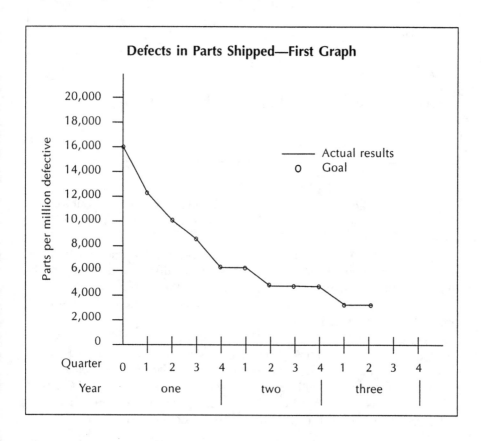

"This one should be familiar to you—I have shown it several times. It displays our actual performance starting two and a half years ago when our defects shipped was 16,000 ppm. Today we are shipping at 3,000 ppm.

"We did not use an internal goal system. Our source of motivation to improve was the customer's specification changes. We reluctantly agreed with the customer's demands. Then we came close to meeting them, but internally kicking and screaming all the way. Over two and a half years, an improvement of 5.3 times is not very impressive.

"We now need to modify the scale on the vertical axis to show our planned progress from 3,000 ppm to 300 ppm in the next twelve months."

Cam put up a new chart (see below).

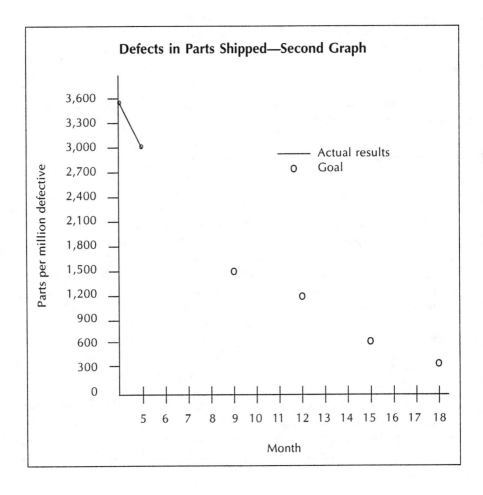

"I have put in the actual data for the last two months and spotted our internal goal of 300 ppm in month 18 with milestone goals along the way.

"Another way of looking at the data is in table form," said Cam, displaying a table on the overhead.

	Number of Returns	Actual Dollars	Percent of Sales	Goal
Product Line A				
Customer Returns—Defective Material				
January	5	1,300	1.3	
February	3	950	0.9	
March	5	1,200	1.1	
First quarter total	**13**	**$3,450**	**1.0%**	**1.1%**
April	4	950	0.9	
May	3	825	0.8	
June	4	775	0.5	
Second quarter total	**11**	**$2,550**	**0.8%**	**1.0%**
July	3	500	0.6	
August	3	450	0.5	
September	2	425	0.5	
Third quarter total	**8**	**$1,375**	**0.5%**	**0.9%**

"This method of collecting and displaying data could be an alternative to a chart, a way to collect data before putting it in a chart, or a way to display more data than can easily be shown in a single chart.

"Now let's look at ways to display a satisfaction index number (see p. 109). We have just shown how to display hard data—that is, an objective number. Now we have to display soft data—a subjective number, an opinion expressed as a number from a satisfaction survey.

"We haven't actually had cause to chart a satisfaction index yet, but this," he said, replacing the table with another chart, "should work."

"Hey," said Ferg, "that's not fair. Don't we get to exceed our goals as well?"

"I just threw that in to make sure you were paying attention. Now, the last method I have to show is kind of a catchall for all those results that are not measured with a goal number." Cam replaced the chart on the overhead with a simple list of processes that had been changed (see p. 109).

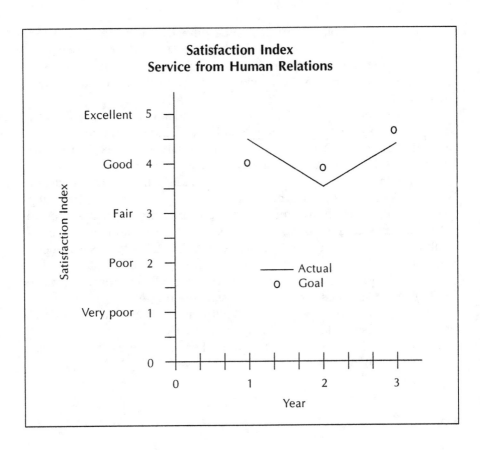

Satisfaction Index
Service from Human Relations

Documented Process Changes

New filing system for administrative assistants installed on 1/14.

New mailing list installed and received final approval on 1/24.

Preventative maintenance procedure established on the critical pieces of equipment in the Concord plant on 1/28.

"So a chart, a table, or a list is to accompany any review," said Carl. In his mind, he was envisioning the instrument panel on a Boeing 747 with a hundred or so instruments—in this case the key results indicators—to tell the pilot all he or she needed to know to fly the plane safely to its destination.

"The leaders of the top five goals and the leaders of the CFTs are to start preparing charts immediately," said Carl. "And, for simplicity's sake, let's call them charts, whether they are charts, tables, or lists. Our job will be to monitor those charts—our key results indicators—all the time.

"I am very pleased with our progress," he said. "Ever since the kickoff, we have stayed right on schedule and have taken another four steps toward Continuous Improvement: we've collected problems and opportunities, we've selected our top five, we've set goals, and we have just established a method for holding everyone accountable for results—not to mention that nearly everyone has gone through Workshop 1.

"The next part we have to cover is to appreciate and reward achievement, so let's see those results forms start pouring in."

As everyone stood to leave, Mary Louise made an announcement. "We wrap up Workshop 1 training this week. All classes are scheduled full, though we might squeeze in a few more here and there. This is the last call to get trained."

MONTH 8

- **Carl's despair at less than 100 percent training attendance**

- **The first official result**

- **Designing ways to appreciate and reward achievement**

Carl was in despair. By now, 100 percent of the people should have attended their first training workshop, but only 85 percent had. He called Harvey as soon as he got the news. "Eighty-five percent!" he moaned. "That's lousy. Everyone knows it's required. The training is good. There is plenty of class space. We've accommodated rescheduling. What is going on?"

"Look," said Harvey, "there are probably hundreds of reasons why 15 percent of the people didn't show up, including 'the dog ate my training manual.' Forget the reasons. Tell the staff your feelings and what you expect from them."

A very somber Carl opened the meeting that week. "I am not at all pleased with 85 percent attendance performance on training. I want 100 percent!"

"Gee, Carl," said Ferg, "85 percent is pretty good. We all worked really hard just to get that."

"I want 100 percent. That's what we agreed on."

No one spoke.

"Look, 100 percent is a *requirement*. Eighty-five percent participation is a flabby response. Pretty soon people will be saying meetings are required, but we don't have to attend them either. Once that happens the whole effort falls apart.

"I will not be tested—100 percent means 100 percent."

Everyone shifted in their seats uncomfortably.

"Now," said Carl, looking at Moe and then at Carol, neither of whom had made it to a training workshop yet, "Mary Louise has scheduled more workshops for the next six weeks. Can I count on you?"

Carol knew all eyes were on her.

"Yes," she said, with a sigh. "I'll attend and I'll get all the field sales-people to attend as well."

"Moe?" Carl looked directly at him.

"I'll go as well," he said, "and I promise that all my people will go too."

"Good," said Carl. "Enough said. Let's move on to how to show appreciation for Continuous Improvement accomplishments."

Before he could say any more, Bill, Cam, and Mary Louise pushed back their chairs and stood up together.

"Carl," said Mary Louise, "would you please stand?"

As Carl rose, Bill walked toward him holding out a sheet of paper. "Our first official result (see p. 113)." Carl's demeanor shifted from wary to pleased.

"This is from one of Cam's first-level CITs," Bill continued. "Cam asked me to read it because he's too bashful. This particular team, the failure analysis CIT, has five members and was among the first to go through Workshop 1—so they got a little jump on everyone else." Bill cleared his throat and began to read.

When he was finished, he handed the form to Carl and everyone applauded.

Carl was beaming. "That is not the biggest fish in the sea," he said, "but it's *our* fish." He then walked around the table shaking hands and saying thank you to Cam, Bill, and Mary Louise.

"Perhaps you should save your thanks for Rosalie and her team," said Jim. "What are the chances of them coming up to tell us specifically what they did?" he asked Cam.

"Pretty good," Cam replied. "I'll go get them."

Within ten minutes the failure analysis CIT, plus their coach, had filed into the conference room amid congratulations.

"What do you want me to say?" asked Rosalie. "Where should I start?"

"Start from the beginning," said Cam.

"Well, we all got our training during the first sessions of the workshop and started our meetings right away. Initially, we met every week for just an hour, but once we got started, we each had additional assignments

---

Results

Team name: *Failure Analysis CIT*   Today's date: *Sept. 14*

Leader: *Rosalie*   Starting date: *Aug. 1*

Members: *Marian, Michael, Haley, Ted, Barbara (trainer)*

Problem or opportunity expressed as a goal:
Currently it is taking twelve weeks to analyze customer returns. Our goal is to analyze product returns and send the customers a report within ten working days of receipt of the returns and to have this in operation within six weeks.

Describe the solution (list the key processes changed, eliminated, or added):
Met with salespeople, receiving, and inspection. Reviewed the old procedure. Developed a new procedure—from sales issuing a return authorization to completion of the process. Returns at receiving are to come to quality within eight hours. After they are logged in, inspection has three days to reinspect. We have the balance of days for analysis, report, and deposition. Have put big red tags on the lots with places for dates.

Results:
As of now our backlog is less than ten days.

Benefits (including, if possible, projected annual savings):
1. *People's time is no longer wasted chasing the status of returns.*
2. *Customers are happier.*

---

outside the meetings. Basically, we just followed the training. We made a list of problems, selected one dealing with product returns, and set a goal."

"What made you choose this particular problem?" asked Jim.

"It was a natural," said Rosalie. "The entire process was screwed up from the time the customer told us our products didn't meet specifications to the time we were able to return a decent product. The customers either weren't aware of our procedures for returns or they simply refused to follow them. In some cases, our own salespeople didn't follow the procedures. We decided it was time to come up with a new method."

"How does it work?" asked Elaine.

"Perhaps Michael should explain his part," said Rosalie, "since he had one of the bright ideas."

"My part was to work with the people in the receiving department," he said. "Before we started Continuous Improvement, they would let the product returns from customers sit in receiving for who knows how long. They'd usually get lost or reshipped uninspected, and sometimes one would actually make it to the inspection department. It all depended on *who* was working when the product came in.

"The solution for my part was really simple. We set up a table and storage space with a red sign overhead that read 'Put customer returns here.' Now, every morning at 8 A.M. one of us goes over to the table, collects everything there, and brings it to our failure-analysis area."

"Do you have your new process flow on the computer?" asked Ferg.

"No," answered Rosalie, "we did it all on paper. We thought about putting it on the computer, but Cam said not to bother because in a year, when the quality is right, there won't be any returns."

"How did you measure your progress?"

"That was Marian's department."

"We wanted to have a new, documented process in place by a certain date," Marian explained. "Part of that process included a tracking note-book to record the date the product came in, the day it should be out, and the day a report actually goes to the customer. It's part of the process, but it also tells us where we stand, which is currently less than ten days from receipt of the product to mailing the analysis report to the customer and deciding the deposition of the return."

"That's just great," said Carl. "You all did a terrific job. Thanks."

After Rosalie's team left, everyone was relieved to see that Carl was in a much better mood. He knew Continuous Improvement was going to work, and that was a huge relief. He now broached the subject of appreciation with renewed vigor.

"As you've seen, people are starting to pull through for us," he said. "The trainers, in particular, have done their job and done it well. So, I'd say the time was right to talk about appreciating and rewarding people.

"Appreciation is a special way of saying 'Thank you. I appreciate what you have done.' A reward is something that has real value to the individual, such as more pay or a bonus. It can also have nonmonetary value, such as a title or special education.

"Our next task," he continued, "is to find ways to let all the people who have contributed know we appreciate what they've done. Now, before I assign a specific action committee for this, I was wondering if you had any ideas."

A short silence ensued. It was broken by Bill, who had a cautionary tale instead of an idea.

"The last company I worked for had a similar companywide excellence program," he said. "There were awards at the department and division levels, with winners for each location. There were also company winners and a grand champion winner. The problem was that this took a lot of energy but made only about 5 percent of the people happy. For every winner there was a large number of losers, and losers don't hustle back to work to solve problems."

"I had a different experience," said Elaine, "in a company about our size, with a president who had real flair."

"Carl has flair," said Jim.

"That's right," said Carl, and everybody laughed. "Go ahead, Elaine, if we can keep the riffraff quiet."

"As I was saying, this guy had flair. When he started Continuous Improvement, he rented ten new Cadillacs and had them parked in ten specially marked spaces. Each month, all the people who had met their performance goals put their names into a hat. Ten names were drawn, and those people each got to drive one of the Caddies for a month."

"How could he afford that?" asked Cam.

"Easy," said Elaine. "Because of Continuous Improvement, he figured the company had saved $2 million in the first six months, and all indications pointed to another $3 million in savings over the next twelve. The Cadillacs were a drop in the bucket compared to that. Besides, it really got people's attention and everyone got involved."

"I like that idea," said Cam, who was thinking he was about due for a new car anyway. "Do we get to pick the options?"

"Let's not get ahead of ourselves," said Carl. "First we need someone to head up the specific action committee on appreciation. Any volunteers?"

Mary Louise raised her hand. "I'll do it," she said.

By the following week, Ferg had prepared, at Carl's request, some ideas on a reward system that might be used for Continuous Improvement performance.

"Rewards come in two basic packages," he said. "Nonfinancial rewards include promotions, more interesting jobs, better working hours, better offices, enhanced titles, prestigious assignments, and special education—something the people want.

"Financial rewards include such things as pay increases, fewer hours worked for the same pay, bonuses, stock payments, use of an automobile, payment of dues to a club, and flying first class.

"In our case, pay increases in particular get a little tricky. Since we are part of a large company, we need to fit into a specific salary pattern. We also need to fit into our industry salary pattern, both as to level of pay and the differential between jobs.

"However, there's nothing to stop us from using any of the nonfinancial rewards I mentioned right now, but we do need to be careful to make this work for us.

"First of all, we should make it a policy that the *only* people promoted are those who value Continuous Improvement and have shown direct involvement in meeting Continuous Improvement goals. Then, when they are promoted, they must be told that one of the main reasons for the promotion was their contribution to Continuous Improvement."

"Good point," said Carl. "I'd like to add something else. I propose that our existing yearly bonus system, which involves only the top fifty people, be amended. For example, if an individual's total bonus works out to be $20,000, then 30 percent, or $6,000, would be earmarked for Continuous Improvement. If this person did an outstanding job on Continuous Improvement, he or she would receive the whole $6,000. However, if the person just went along for the ride, he or she might get only $2,000.

"Somewhere down the line I'd also like to see some kind of bonus system for everyone," said Carl, "not just the top 7 percent. However, I will have to find the right time and place to broach this subject with my two bosses.

"For the time being, let's just be aware that we have to reward people with top performance both financially and nonfinancially regardless of how they fit into the company's hierarchy."

On the way out of the meeting, Mary Louise cornered Carl and asked if he was aware that the executive administrative assistants had formed a first-level CIT.

"I knew something was going on," said Carl, "but I don't know the details."

"Your very own administrative assistant is the ringleader. I've even assigned a trainer to her team."

"How's it going?"

"So far, so good," said Mary Louise. "They have lots of mutual issues such as covering for each other when away from their desks, conference room scheduling, getting supplies, using the fax machines, and making travel plans. They're identifying work processes, selecting problems, and setting goals—everything a regular first-level CIT would do. Looks like you've created a monster."

Carl was delirious. "This is a monster I can live with."

Mary Louise was the only member of the executive CIT on the appreciation specific action committee. The rest of the members came from all levels and all parts of the company. After two meetings, however, Mary Louise decided they couldn't proceed without some guidelines—parameters from the executive CIT.

At the next executive CIT meeting, she wrote all the ideas her committee had generated on chart paper and posted them on the walls of the conference room. Then she asked the group for help in eliminating the ideas that were not acceptable. The discussion was lively as she started crossing things off the list with a thick crayon. When they were done, only one-fourth of the items remained, all acceptable to the CIT. With this list in hand, Mary Louise went back to her committee and together they designed a complete appreciation effort to present to the executive CIT.

At the last executive CIT meeting of the month, Mary Louise unveiled an appreciation effort for the team's approval. She stepped to the chart stand and wrote, "Say thank you."

"Say it often," Mary Louise said. "Say it with adjectives. Say it with feelings. Say it privately and publicly. Say it to anyone who deserves it. Say it without conditions. Say it face to face. Say it in a handwritten memo. Just say thank you.

"To that end, I have a little gift for each of you." She pulled a stack of five-by-eight-inch notepads from her bag and passed one to each person in the room. Each sheet had "I appreciate you" printed at the top. "Use these liberally," she said. "I have lots more.

"More formal appreciation," Mary Louise continued, "will be given at special ceremonies by Carl in the form of a bronze pin for the first award an individual receives in a year, a silver pin for the second award in the same year, and a gold pin for the third award in the same year. Members of any team that met its goal are eligible to receive one, provided they turn in a completed results form signed by the manager or supervisor of the team leader. There will be no distinction between big, difficult accomplishments and small, modest accomplishments. If there is a real whopper, the executive CIT can, at its own discretion, do something special.

"We also thought that individual departments could do something special for appreciation recipients," Mary Louise continued. "Money, for example, could be allocated for an office party, hats, T-shirts, or what have you."

"How about a Caddie for the fourth award in a year?" asked Moe.

"Enough on the Cadillacs," said Carl. "I don't have that much flair."

"As a matter of fact," said Mary Louise, "my committee wants to know what kind of a whopper it would take to get you to do a real live song and dance for us, Carl. I hear you've got quite a voice."

Carl scratched his head for a minute while everyone wondered whether he'd take the bait. "Okay," he finally said. "If we hit no more than 5 percent missed product deliveries to promise date every week for the sixteen consecutive weeks that follow the goal date—month 23—on the order-to-shipment tracking system, I will give a first-class, public song and dance!

"No flair and a damned fool. Woe is me. Let's take a break before the staff meeting," Carl said, and then he held up a hand. "Hold it, I forgot to give the look-ahead: month 9, more on training; month 10, more on resistance; month 11, an update on communications; and month 12, first anniversary review."

MONTH 9

- ■ **More on training everyone**
- ■ **Jason's maintenance project**

Mary Louise circulated a list of the 110 people who still needed to attend a workshop. She sent it to each person on the list and to his or her manager or supervisor. Attached was a schedule of workshops with openings still available. She updated the list every week and made sure Carl received a copy.

She had organized the list by grouping untrained people under the name of the appropriate executive CIT member. That way, Carl knew who to buttonhole in the hallway. He was relentless.

Mary Louise also hung a nine-foot-high drawing of a thermometer in the cafeteria labeled "Workshop 1 Attendance—Goal 100 Percent." The large red stripe up the middle of the thermometer was extended whenever someone was trained.

"The thermometer has really got people buzzing," said Ferg, "but there are still some skeptics. I heard one person say, 'They'll never get them all.'"

"Oh, yes we will," said Mary Louise. "I'm going after every last one of them."

By the middle of the month, there were only seventeen people left to train. By the next week, all eyes were on the thermometer. The following Monday, only seven people were left; their names and units were known to everyone.

Six of them went through the course on Tuesday and Wednesday. The only person left was at home caring for her ill husband. Undaunted, Mary Louise sent a trainer to her home on Thursday.

By Friday afternoon, a large group, including Carl and most of the executive CIT, had gathered around the thermometer. At 4 P.M. the trainer called in and said the last person had just completed the course. A huge cheer resounded through the cafeteria as one of the warehouse workers lifted Mary Louise onto his shoulders so she could paint the red stripe all the way up to the 100 percent mark.

The enthusiasm was contagious, and spirits companywide seemed to soar. Moe came to the next executive CIT meeting with a bulging brown paper bag full of three-inch-diameter buttons for everyone.

"Do it right the first time," they read, "no matter how many times it takes you."

Things were looking pretty good, thought Carl, but he wanted a report from the field just to be sure. So, at the next executive CIT meeting, he asked Mary Louise what the trainers were saying about the managers and supervisors who were leading problem-solving teams.

"Most of them are doing a very good job," she said, "but some are just fair and a handful are awful."

"In what way?" asked Carl.

"Well, some of them don't bother coming to the meetings, and if they do come, they don't participate. A few pooh-pooh the whole concept, and one or two solve the problems themselves and then tell the people what to do."

"Stop right there!" said Carl. "I want you to give the names of those people to the appropriate person in this room. Then I strongly suggest that each of you find a way to remove them as team leaders until they can be brought up to speed or permanently replaced."

"Don't you think that's a little tough?" asked Jim.

"No, I don't," said Carl. "Keeping them on sends a terrible message. It tells people we don't care how they are treated. It tells them we care only about ramming Continuous Improvement down their throats. That is unacceptable. Period. End of sentence."

"Well, one of the things I thought we should do is to get a team leader course under way," said Mary Louise, "say in about two months."

"Shouldn't it be sooner if we're having trouble with our leaders now?" asked Bill.

"We're really only having serious trouble with a handful. The rest are doing quite nicely. I think the team leader training will be more helpful after they've struggled a bit."

"You obviously have something in mind already," said Carl.

"As a matter of fact I do. Harvey and I have been talking. We would start such a session by listing all the things that make a lousy meeting.

We'd have everyone contribute—generate a long list. At the end of the first hour, we'd just say that the way to have a good meeting is not to do any of these things.

"Then we'd make three more lists. One would be the kinds of things they are doing in their meetings that are effective, another the things they are doing that are not effective, and the third would be other problems, issues, concerns, feelings, and gripes. We would spend time discussing the lists before creating the final list of 'Good Practices for Problem-Solving Leaders.' The whole thing shouldn't take more than about four hours, and by the end of the session, we can expect that each team leader will leave with two or three things that they know they must improve.

"I'd like to get these under way in the next six weeks for all problem-solving team leaders," continued Mary Louise. "Harvey will be the session leader."

"While we're on the subject of training," said Cam, "I've got another idea. Jeff, our statistics person, has offered to teach some basic statistics to the nonengineering people in the company. I think this is a great idea and should be required for everyone."

"Let's think about that," said Carl. "It might not be a bad idea. Since training is obviously on everyone's mind today, perhaps it's a good time for Mary Louise to fill us in on Workshop 2."

"Let me refresh your memory," she said. "It's very similar to the first workshop in that there is a problem to be solved from a short scenario— Pete's Puppy Pen Case. This time, however, people will learn the rest of the twenty-two techniques not covered in Workshop 1 and will diagram a poor work-flow process, changing it into an optimum work-flow process by the end of the workshop. It's also shorter than Workshop 1—six hours instead of nine.

"Right now, I have them scheduled to start two weeks from today, with time slots available over the following six weeks. By the end of Workshop 2, everyone will be thoroughly trained in basic problem solving. And, by the way, the thermometer will be turned on!"

"What about new hires?" Carol asked Ferg. "How will they get the problem-solving training?"

"We've already taken care of that," he said. "Two hours of the eight-hour introduction to Clear Run is devoted to Continuous Improvement. Among other things, we agree on a date for them to attend Workshop 1, which would be about six weeks after they start work."

"Yes," said Mary Louise. "We haven't disbanded Workshop 1 entirely. We still offer it for special circumstances such as this."

After the meeting, Bill approached Carl to talk about Jason, a relative newcomer to Clear Run who was hired eighteen months before as head of maintenance. Bill thought Carl might like to hear about one of Jason's projects.

"Why not have him tell everyone?" asked Carl. "Invite him to our next executive CIT meeting."

Jason was clearly a little nervous when he walked into the room the following week, but after a round of introductions he could sense that everyone was on his side. "We have just completed an internal customer survey that rated our work as poor," he began. "Now, we don't agree with that. We think most of these people's problems are their own fault. But, since we're supposed to believe the customer is always right, we've got to fix this. So, with some strong encouragement from Bill here, we set a goal to go from 'poor' to 'good' within six months.

"To do this, we had the following printed on the back of each work order." He held up a work order and read aloud: "Did the person who performed the work do it right the first time? Was it done within the published allowed time? Was the person doing the work courteous? If the answer to any of the above is no, please contact the maintenance supervisor.

"This has had an immediate impact toward earning us that good rating. The deal is that no maintenance people will go out to do anything until they really understand what's required by the person who requested the work or until they know how to do the job and can take the proper tools and, if possible, the needed replacement parts."

"How is it going so far?" asked Carl.

"I've already received some calls from our customers complimenting us," said Jason. "We're even thinking of changing our goal from 'good' to 'excellent.' The maintenance people feel positive about it as well. They were getting tired of people always complaining for no good reason.

"I just want to say one more thing," he added. "We were doing so-called Continuous Improvement in the company I came from. But the focus was on simple problems such as relocating drinking fountains. You might say we were out to slay field mice rather than dragons. It apparently died a merciful death about six months after I left. When I heard about us starting Continuous Improvement here, I seriously considered taking a hike; I'd just escaped from that foolishness. But, I've got to tell you, this is working out pretty well. Give me and my gang about two more months and we'll have the best maintenance crew in the valley."

MONTH 10

- **More on resistance**

- **Moe's progress**

- **Harvey helps Carol**

- **Carl ponders his time spent on Continuous Improvement**

By the start of month 10, Carl was really beginning to witness a change that seemed to encompass all aspects of the organization. People stopped him wherever they saw him to simply say thanks.

"We always wanted to help, but nobody ever asked us," said one.

"Some of us used to check our brains at the front door because you never used them," said another.

Carl was both delighted and surprised, as he had expected nothing but resistance from the first-level people.

"You've dumped on these people for years, when all along they've wanted to help," said Harvey, patting Carl on the back. "Now that you've asked for help, you're getting it—and they're finally getting the recognition they deserve. People will do anything for you when they are properly led."

Harvey continued, "I still think you'll get the most resistance from your managers and your professional and technical people, rather than from the first-level people."

This was confirmed at the next "Coffee with Carl" session. "The thing I like about this method," said a first-level person, "is that we talk about what people do—the process—not about the people themselves. This takes the blame away from the people, so they don't get defensive and become unwilling to participate. Rather than hiding behind the problem, they talk about it. It's beautiful. We've made more progress in a few weeks than we've made in years."

However, one person did mention that, on occasion, the problem really did rest with an individual. Carl explained that in that case, it was up to the person in charge to help the individual responsible with job training and counseling or to assign the person to different work.

With resistance still on his mind, Carl decided to see Bill to find out whether he was seeing any resistance to the effort.

"Yeah," Bill said, "I've got a few managers and supervisors who do not have faith; they are not in the wheelbarrow."

"Faith? Wheelbarrow?" Carl asked.

"Sure," said Bill. "If you saw someone push a wheelbarrow along a rope stretched over the Grand Canyon a few times, you would *believe* it could be done. *Faith,* on the other hand, is when you actually get into the wheelbarrow.

"Unfortunately, I don't think any more counseling or special training will work with a couple of these guys. The job is simply more than they can handle. And I have two other supervisors who are darn good but who are very negative on Continuous Improvement."

"Can we move any of these people to other jobs where they would be a better fit?" asked Carl.

"I don't think so," said Bill.

"I hate to fire anyone," said Carl, "but if we have to, we have to."

Fortunately, within a month four of those with whom Bill was having difficulty had found other jobs and left of their own accord. The fifth, it turned out, never wanted to be a supervisor to begin with, so Bill put him in a nonsupervisory position, where he was much happier. Carl was relieved. The problem was solved and they hadn't had to fire anyone.

Moe was having good days followed by bad days. He had three small hornets' nests of angry engineers, mad because they had to attend training and work on solving problems. Most of the engineers were running with their heads down—just pounding away with long hours rather than taking the time to figure out better ways to work. Moe was spending 25 percent of his time hiring new people and trying to hang onto those he had because the job market had tightened up as a boom developed.

But he was making progress. He hired a project management expert on the major new product to help with scheduling and to identify bottlenecks. The Continuous Improvement system helped clear some air with the production engineers, operators, and purchasing. Some prior difficult problems were solved. Moe simply listened to some of the disgruntled engineers, and they started to feel better. He also helped hammer out the method of transferring the new product from development to production by encouraging his people and Bill's people to develop an orderly transfer process.

Over the next month, Moe's mood began to improve appreciably, and he was even beginning to sound like his old cocky self. Everyone knew things must be going right, for a change, on the major new product, so no one was surprised when he and Carl laid a little incentive on the new product engineers.

"If you meet the scheduled date," Moe told them, "Carl and I will take you to the finest restaurant in town. You may order anything you want, but Carl and I will eat beans—cold beans." Everyone started to clap, but Moe held up his hand to silence them. "However, if you do *not* meet the scheduled date, you will eat the cold beans and the two of us will order from the menu. Deal?"

The resounding applause let Moe know he had one.

When everyone else had left for the day, Carl turned to Moe and asked, "Think they want to see us suffer?"

"They're going to die trying."

The next issue of the Continuous Improvement newsletter carried the following lead line: "Cold Beans for Carl and Moe? You Bet."

Carol was now a true believer in Continuous Improvement, particularly since she learned that half the errors leading to customer administrative credits stemmed from her own department. Orders were now being entered in the field sales offices, which were more familiar with the customers' paperwork. This also made it easier to track accountability. As a result, the order-editor positions created years ago were no longer necessary, and those people were transferred to other jobs.

Carol now needed some help in defining other significant problems to work on. Harvey suggested that she gather together some local salespeople, inside sales administrators, and some market specialists from Jim's department to meet with him and Carol.

A few days later, they all assembled in the sales conference room. Harvey presided over the meeting and began by stepping up to the chart paper and writing, "Work-flow processes in sales." Then he turned to the group and said, "Let's think of the processes of your work. Here's one." He turned back to the chart paper and wrote "supplying samples."

"This is a process that starts when the customer requests the sample and ends when the customer receives the sample. Do you have any others?"

"Answering inquiries and sending out literature," said one.

"Handling sales leads," said another. Harvey wrote furiously as they kept coming.

"Teaching new salespeople the product line."

"Sales calls."

"Finding out how Clear Run's products are being used."

"Finding out the customers' future needs."

"Introducing a new product."

When they were done, Harvey stood back from the chart paper and explained, "Each of these is a process. And hidden in any one of them may be a problem that needs to be solved or an opportunity waiting to be discovered."

At that point Harvey handed each person three sheets of paper labeled "Concerning Our Customers" (see p. 127), "Concerning Our Suppliers" (see p. 127), and "Concerning Our Own Work" (see p. 128), each containing a list of questions. "Teams that are stuck because they can't find a worthy problem or opportunity to work on could start by asking themselves these questions," said Harvey. "I won't read them to you, but I think if you spend a little time thinking about them, you'll soon come up with some new problems or opportunities.

"Now, you're not expected to spend a great deal of time writing answers to each and every question. They are primarily catalysts—something to start you thinking. If you spend a few minutes with these lists and think about the processes we outlined earlier, I think you will all have something to contribute at your next problem-solving meeting."

As the Continuous Improvement pace eased a bit, Carl seemed to have more time to think as he drove to and from work. He certainly had put in more than two hours a week since starting Continuous Improvement more than nine months ago, he thought. He hadn't kept track, but four to five hours a week was more like it. Since he put in some fifty hours a week, Continuous Improvement was taking up almost 10 percent of his time. Was it worth it?

Nine months ago Clear Run was just starting to see a boom time on the horizon. Now the orders were really rolling in. The projection made just a week ago indicated sales would grow 30 percent in the next twelve months and they would need to hire 15 percent more people rather than the 10 percent they had anticipated.

Concerning Our Customers

- Can we identify our customers—that is, the people or groups who are the recipients of our work?

- Can we identify their needs?

- Do we work out requirements with them?

- Do we meet all our promises to them?

- Are they pleased with our overall performance? What do they say, specifically?

- What problems do we have with them?

- Do we explain our capabilities to them? Explain how to use us?

- What can we do to make it easier for our customers to do their jobs better?

Concerning Our Suppliers

- Can we identify our suppliers—that is, the people or groups who provide us with material and information?

- Do they understand our needs and why we have these needs?

- Do we work out requirements with them?

- Do they meet all their requirements with us? If not, do we discuss this with them?

- Are we pleased with their performance?

- What problems do we have with them?

- Do we ask them about their capabilities?

- Have we explained to them what they could do to make our work easier and to help us serve our customers better?

Concerning Our Own Work

■ What hindrances do we have in doing our own jobs right the first time?

■ Do we see opportunities to do our work faster?

■ Are we working on the right things?

■ Do all the things we do add value for our inside and outside customers?

■ Could some part of our work be done better by somebody else?

■ Is the process needed at all? Should it be done elsewhere? Could the steps be simplified? Could some steps be combined or eliminated? Is it error-proof? Could new techniques be applied? Does it use too much space? Could the work be done faster? Is there variability in completion time?

■ How much time do we waste?

■ What are the reasons our time is wasted, either by our actions or the actions of others?

■ How much work do we do over?

■ Why do we have to do work over?

■ Do we know anybody who does this kind of work and operates very efficiently? Have we talked to them?

This would take yet another chunk of Carl's time He tried to do some quick calculations. A lot of his time was devoted to meetings with the parent organization in New York and Europe. By the time he factored in all the time spent traveling there and back, preparing for the meetings, discussing the outcomes on his return, and the loads of visiting bigwigs who had to be treated properly, it accounted for about 20 percent of his time.

Another 30 percent was spent on customer issues—visits to and from customers and distributors, handling problems, finding new opportunities, discussing pricing policies, learning about competitors, and so on.

The balance, 40 percent, was spent working on operations and attending the monthly meetings with the five major segments of the business to discuss actual sales, costs and earnings versus budgets and business plans, product reviews, personnel issues, and persuading people to stay with Clear Run.

Of all of his time, fully 15 percent, he figured, was wasted. Wasted dealing with angry customers and trying to satisfy them. Wasted listening to upset and frustrated Clear Run people who could not get done what they wanted to get done. Wasted putting Band-Aids on the same problems over and over again. Wasted in poorly run meetings.

He felt he could reduce the time he spent on Continuous Improvement to two hours a week if he didn't include the time spent on "Coffee with Carl" or his general quarterly meetings, as they were implemented before Continuous Improvement.

As he drove along, he calculated: two hours out of fifty hours a week is 4 percent. But, he thought to himself, "It should end up saving me at least half of the time that is now wasted, or 7.5 percent. So I should end up ahead of the game."

His mood was dimmed later that day during "Coffee with Carl." Two of the ten people there were clearly jaded—convinced their bosses wouldn't change and that Continuous Improvement wouldn't work. He drove home that evening thinking of Harvey's observations on resistance and Calvin Coolidge's words on persistence:

"Nothing in the world can take the place of persistence. Talent will not; nothing is more common than unsuccessful men with talent. Genius will not; unrewarded genius is almost a proverb. Education will not; the world is full of educated derelicts. Persistence and determination alone are omnipotent. The slogan 'Press On' has solved, and always will solve, the problems of the human race."

MONTH 11

- **Communications update**

- **Policy, practice, and procedure hindrances**

- **Experts**

- **The first appreciation ceremony**

- **ISO 9000, QS-9000, and the MBNQA**

It was now seven months since the big kickoff meeting and Jim's specific action committee on communication had not slowed down one bit. The newsletter, *Clear Run to Number One,* was being published every two weeks and was doing a decent job of keeping everyone informed. The issue that came out right after the kickoff covered the meeting with stories and photographs from top to bottom. The name was chosen after a companywide contest. The ten finalists were given the task of selecting the name from the ten entries they had submitted. The person who submitted the winning entry received a dinner for two at the Fairmont Hotel.

They had also put the video of the big kickoff meeting, the kickoff for the night people, and the kickoff in Concord to good use. It was edited down to forty-five minutes and made available for people who could not attend the kickoff, new hires, and customers. For one week it ran continuously on a television in the cafeterias in Sudbury and Concord.

But what Jim wanted to talk about today was *Clear Run to Number One.*

"This is our major communication vehicle," he told the group. "Every issue focuses on what is actually happening in Continuous Improvement. I hope you agree with me that the content is complete—the trainer selection, Workshop 1, Mary Louise's thermometer caper, the top five goals and assignments, how the first-level CITs will operate, and why people might be resistant to change.

"We've also included pictures of people, comments by people, and letters to Carl, and we don't neglect coverage of the high points of 'Coffee with Carl' sessions, the monthly policy meetings, Carl's quarterly meetings, and any other special meetings. Later this month, we will have full coverage of the first appreciation ceremony, and you will start to see more and more ANs."

"What are ANs?" asked Cam.

"ANs are the five-by-eight-inch 'I appreciate you' notes. We decided to cover them in the newsletter and thus inspire more of them to be given—person to person.

"The newsletter has also mentioned Carl's pending public song and dance, and a few weeks ago we featured the cold beans bet. That reminds me—I have a little gift for each of you," he said, pulling two brand-new can openers from his briefcase and handing one to Carl and one to Moe. "These might come in handy with dinner."

"If I end up using this," said Carl, "I'll have it bronzed and framed."

"Better start looking for a place to hang it," laughed Jim. "Now, for the time being we'll continue to publish *Clear Run to Number One* and our regular newsletter separately. But once Continuous Improvement is embedded in the company, a year or so from now, we should think about combining the two.

"We have also supplied each department and unit with a bulletin board, like this one (see p. 133)," he said, balancing a huge bulletin board on the edge of the table. "This is what I hope they will look like about twelve months from now. This one is from my department, marketing.

"As you can see, we can use this to monitor attendance at meetings, for those who wish to. We can also use it to list the problems that are currently being worked on, to post the most recently completed results forms, to show *key performance indicators,* to list pending problems and opportunities, and to display appreciation citations with photographs of the team members. The idea is to let each team track its own progress and to inform everyone else in the company about what is happening in a particular unit."

Marketing CIT Bulletin Board

ATTENDANCE

names	JAN	FEB	MAR
～	1 2 3 4	1 2 3 4	1 2 3 4
～	x x x x	x x	
～	x o x o	x o	
～	x x x x	x x	
～	x x x x	x x	
～	x o x x	o x	
%	87 87 90 95 92 75		
rating	4 3 4 5 4 2		

KEY PERFORMANCE INDICATORS

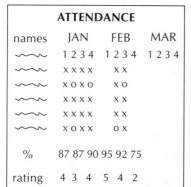
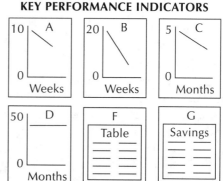

UNDER WAY

results to goals	results to goals

3 MOST RECENTLY COMPLETED

results to goals	results to goals	results to goals

LIST OF PENDING PROBLEMS/ OPPORTUNITIES

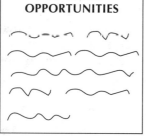

APPRECIATION CITATION

appreciation citation	appreciation citation	appreciation citation

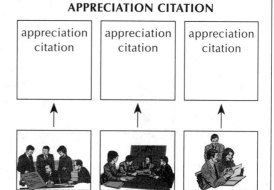

"That's your instrument panel, your chart room," said Harvey.

"For the marketing department anyway," replied Jim. "Each department should have its own.

"The last thing I want to mention today is that our very first appreciation ceremony will be held later this month, as will the executive CIT's first anniversary. Keep your ears tuned for more information about both of these events."

As Carl drove home that evening, he thought with pleasure about the day's meeting, the progress they were making, and the feeling of camaraderie that was developing. He hated to turn his attention from such pleasant reverie, but there was an iceberg to deal with. An iceberg of policy, practices with a controlling management style, and procedure hindrances—all mostly underwater and unseen. "If we pick away at a few items at a time, we won't end up like the *Titanic*," he thought.

Carl had already asked Elaine to form a CFT to unravel the subject. She in turn had asked Daniela, who was in charge of Clear Run's financial documentation and procedures, to lead a CFT composed of specialists from the engineering, quality, and human resources departments. They had been meeting twice a week and were now ready to give a report to the executive CIT. Next week would be soon enough, thought Carl, to start chipping away at the iceberg.

"Using the information from the organizationwide surveys, material from our files, and conversations with key people," said Daniela, "we were able to split the subject into two categories.

"The first category includes mandated, for want of a better word, policies, practices, and procedures of a legal, safety, or financial nature such as wage and hour laws; fair employment practices; fire, health, and safety regulations; internal wage and salary policy; legal contracts; legal behavior; and sound accounting principles.

"The second category, which we're calling unmandated policies, practices, and procedures, includes everything else—for example, the approved levels for spending certain amounts of money; personal performance reviews; the number, length, and content of meetings; the procedures for requesting capital spending; all manufacturing and quality documentation; the budget system; the four-year plan; business review practices; and the controlling nature of the company."

"Once we tallied up all the policies, practices, and procedures," added Elaine, "we were astounded at the amount. Most of them are necessary but could be handled more efficiently."

"Can you give us a couple of examples?" asked Bill.

"The level of spending authority hasn't changed in seven years and is far too low by today's standards," answered Daniela. "We have three authority levels, and therefore three required signatures, to buy any item over a hundred dollars!

"The signatures needed on engineering change orders haven't been reviewed in more than ten years. And my committee members from engineering say it takes forever to get any changes approved."

"Another is poor meetings," added Elaine. "Everyone on our committee complained about such things as no agendas, not starting and ending on time, not having the right people in attendance, and not reaching a decision on the subject at hand."

"And what do you mean by the 'controlling nature of the company'?" asked Jim.

There was a long silence, which was finally broken by Harvey. "As an outsider, I might be able to describe this a bit better. It seems that a lot of supervisors, and middle and upper managers, are afraid to make decisions, so they keep asking for approval higher up. I believe this attitude derives from a style seen at the top—a style that says, 'A budget is a budget and a goal is a goal, and not meeting either won't be tolerated.' This makes management people cautious in setting budgets and goals and timid about making daily decisions."

"Do you have an example?" asked Bill, somewhat incredulously.

"Sure. One of your top lieutenants carries a black book containing each of his subordinate's budgets, goals, and current commitments. He checks on them daily. Consequently, they ask his permission just to refill their coffee cups."

"Oh," said Bill, sheepishly.

That was enough for Carl. "This is all I can handle in one dose," he said. "This is hitting pretty close to home, and I've got to go think about these things. It is obvious that I must personally lead the revolution in management style around here, but we must all work together to remove the hindrances caused by the policies, practices, and procedures currently in place."

By the next meeting, Carl had a few ideas. "I've got three suggestions," he began. "Elaine, would you direct your CFT to look at the mandated stuff and make appropriate recommendations for improvements? I'd also like you to present us with a proposal for new, more appropriate levels of spending authority.

"Next, I would like Bill, Ferg, and Jim to each form a CFT on conducting good meetings. Apply some of the techniques the leaders discovered in their four-hour leader training session. Give us your thoughts in six weeks—and keep to the point.

"The last one is mine. There is no question that I have set a controlling style."

"Hear, hear," muttered the four who had just been issued new assignments.

"I have got to examine this closely," continued Carl, "and figure out what to do, because I really don't *know* how to fix it.

"One last thought. Think of policy, practice, and procedure hindrances as an iceberg that we can only reduce by chipping away at it. No blasting. No towing it to the equator to melt. Just chipping away."

Ever since their inception, Carl had always attended the monthly project reviews of the order-to-shipment tracking system. It would, everyone hoped, revolutionize how the company used paperwork and computers—the latest technology available—for everything from entering orders to shipping and billing.

After one particular meeting, Robin, the head of the consulting team hired to install the new method, and Carl met for coffee. "To think of all the production planners that I replaced over the years for incompetence," said Carl, "only to discover now that it was the *system* that was incompetent."

"Times have changed," said Robin. "Things are now so sophisticated with software, computer hardware, and the thrust for doing things faster that good production planners don't have the skills required to design the systems they need."

"Does that mean," asked Carl, "that I am in the clutches of experts in every field?"

"Think of it," said Robin. "The captain of a battleship couldn't design one, and the designer couldn't command one."

Carl looked glum.

"Cheer up," said Robin. "When you were a boy, your family doctor attended to all your ills. Now you go to specialists and get much better medicine. It's the same thing in business."

By the end of the month, twenty-seven teams had turned in results forms, and the cafeteria could barely hold the two hundred people who squeezed in for the first Continuous Improvement appreciation ceremony. The honorees were invited to arrive early and sit at the tables, while the overflow stood along the four walls. Everyone shared in the refreshments that had been provided.

Music was blaring from two speakers as Carl and Bill tiptoed by the video-camera operator and stepped onto a platform that had been erected by the maintenance staff. Carl gave a brief welcome and then turned the microphone over to Bill who, reading from the results forms, gave the accomplishments of each team from operations as the members stepped up to the platform. Carl and Bill shook each person's hand in turn and thanked them personally as the audience clapped and cheered. They would receive their certificates and pins later, at a department meeting.

When all the teams from operations had received their recognition, Carol stepped up to acknowledge the teams from sales. And so it went for a full hour, with each member of the executive CIT extending appreciation to at least one problem-solving team. As Carl watched, he realized that this was his moment—his and the entire executive CIT's. It was quite an accomplishment, all in less than twelve months, from a dead start with three reluctant executives.

The next day, Carl got a call from Bill. "The appreciation ceremony was positive proof to Cam and me that the company is ready to do ISO 9000 in a decent way."

"What do you mean 'do ISO 9000 properly'? I thought we already had approval."

"We do have approval but, as you know, we're right on the margin of becoming disapproved. We've done the minimum. It's time we did it in a first-class manner."

"Don't you think we should discuss this with the executive CIT first?" asked Carl.

"I'm not opposed to explaining what we're up to," said Bill, "but, per our discussion last week on making decisions, we are proceeding."

"Touché," said Carl. "Thanks for the call."

ISO 9000 is an international standard that assures a customer or client that an organization will deliver products and services consistent with agreed-upon specifications. Many companies in the United States and abroad require ISO 9000 approval from their suppliers.

Doing ISO 9000 properly would set Clear Run up to receive QS-9000 approval and then the grand master, the Malcolm Baldrige National Quality Award (MBNQA), which was presented annually to just a few organizations in the United States. To receive the MBNQA, a company must demonstrate business practices that, when shared with other organizations, enhance the competitiveness of the United States as a whole. It was extremely prestigious and had always seemed beyond the reach of Clear Run—until now.

Carl called Harvey right away. "Well," said Harvey, "QS-9000 shouldn't be a problem because you're already using the essence of it on the engine-control project."

"That's right," thought Carl, remembering that QS-9000 had, in fact, been developed by a Chrysler/Ford/General Motors task force with the goal of preventing defects and reducing variation and waste in the supply chain. It was a guarantee, essentially, that the company in question had a sound fundamental quality system and was extremely competent in the field of Continuous Improvement.

"But," continued Harvey, "even though everything you are doing will lead to applying for the MBNQA, you better wait until you have some more solid accomplishments—such as meeting and surpassing some of your top five goals—before you take it on."

Carl could hardly wait.

MONTH 12

- **Another survey of people's opinions**
- **The executive CIT is upset**
- **P.H.C. relationship**
- **Carl's first-year anniversary talk**

It was the beginning of the last month of the first year of Continuous Improvement, and Carl was getting his thoughts in order for his talk to the mid-level CITs. He wanted to take a look at the entire organization and ferret out any issues of concern. With that in mind, he asked Ferg to present a report on people's attitudes toward Continuous Improvement.

Consequently, Ferg asked the executive team members to conduct another Survey of People's Opinions and collect the data in their respective departments so he could compare the results with those collected eight months earlier.

"Overall," he told the executive CIT, after tabulating all the data, "the ratings are somewhat better. The only surprise was statement five: 'The people who give me work, supply me with instructions, inspect my work, and receive my work know what they are doing.' The answers clustered around 2.0, which meant that people mildly disagreed. That might be expected, given the heightened awareness of internal customers and suppliers.

"The answers to question eight, 'What problems do you have in doing your work correctly the first time?' and question nine, 'In what ways could the organization be better?' were generally less critical of management. Most respondents took the opportunity to point out operational problems instead.

"There were a number of comments that indicated resistance to Continuous Improvement or skepticism in its ability to help the company. Other than that, the random comments about top management were about 80 percent complimentary and 20 percent uncomplimentary."

The members of the executive CIT were obviously upset by any criticism leveled at them, no matter how vague, and the fur flew around the table until Harvey held up his hand. "Cool down," he said, "this is normal during a change. It will take time before you are loved and revered."

"Yeah," said Bill, "but we've worked damn hard on this. Don't they see what's going on?"

"They do," answered Harvey. "The problem is that some of you, or the managers just under you, are doing some things that aren't consistent with Continuous Improvement."

"Like what?"

"Well, I have heard about shipping off-specification parts."

"The customer approved that," spurted Cam.

"Even so, they were off-specification. But you're not the only one to blame. Problem-solving meetings have been canceled because something hot had just come up. And one department still hasn't managed to start and stop its meetings on time.

"They're watching you carefully, and any deviation from perfection will catch their attention."

"What are we supposed to do?" asked Elaine. "We can't be perfect."

"People know that, but you have to acknowledge it. If you deviate from good practices, explain why, and tell them how and when you're going to get back on track. Make sure they understand that you haven't forgotten your commitment to Continuous Improvement, and they won't forget theirs."

"Ferg, thank you again for keeping us up-to-the-minute on people's opinions," said Carl.

"Does anybody have any other issues to discuss—good or bad?"

Bill raised his hand next. "I've gotten a few questions about spending money to solve problems and getting permission to make changes. I've told people that the company procedures are to be followed, but I'm beginning to wonder if that's the best way to handle this." He could see an immediate look of concern on Elaine's face.

"What if a team proposes a very expensive solution to a problem?" he continued. "A solution we don't think is appropriate or worthwhile. If we turn them down, won't we turn them off?"

"A solution shouldn't get that far if it's inappropriate," said Elaine. "A sponsor or manager should be staying close to teams that are working on projects that could require a lot of expenditures. As the solutions unfold, the team should be told that any capital proposal or addition of people must be justified by its benefits per our company policy."

"Then it's like we operate now, on capital appropriation," said Bill.

"Exactly," said Elaine.

Next, Carol had an issue with some of the results that were being turned in.

"Some are so thin that if they were soup, you'd see right through them, while others are so thick that a spoon would stand up in them. It doesn't seem fair to appreciate them all in the same way. In fact, if we expect everyone to aspire to tougher problems, we might be shooting ourselves in the foot."

"I agree," said Cam. "Why can't we have a review board to judge the strength of the results and issue appreciation accordingly?"

"I don't see it that way at all," said Elaine. "Appreciation is just an elaborate, flowery way of saying thank you."

"Years ago," said Ferg, "I worked in a glass factory. We had fifteen hundred people working three shifts a day, seven days a week. Whenever an operator on one of the big hot-glass machines broke a record for output on his eight-hour shift, his boss gave him a cigar. When he lit up in the cafeteria, everyone in the plant knew of his accomplishment. It was a ten-cent cigar."

"They probably all got up and left, too," said Elaine.

"Oh, oh, I forgot. Cigars are not so politically correct right now. But that was back in the days when a husband gave cigars to his male friends and chocolates to his female friends when his wife had a baby."

"Not any more, Ferg," said Carol. "Today he would give cigars to the women as well or be called sexist."

"Hold it," said Carl, "we're digressing from the subject. Let's not worry about content at this time. We can encourage teams to choose tougher problems or opportunities once we get rolling. For the time being, a little appreciation will go a long way."

Bill said, "I agree. The other day Moe stopped by our group, after we'd made the first hundred samples of the major new product, and simply said thank you to each person who had worked on the project. That made us *all* feel wonderful, particularly after all the differences we've had."

Carol could see she was outnumbered, but she wanted the last word anyway. "Okay, okay," she said. "I'll settle for Carl using a little, tiny, thin voice for small accomplishments at the appreciation ceremonies and a big, deep, booming voice for big accomplishments!"

"If we're on general issues," said Ferg, "I've got one."

"Shoot," said Carl.

"We've talked about charts and key results indicators together. Are they the same?"

"Not really," said Carl. "Charts are used for tracking progress toward any goal. Key results indicators is a term for the most important and significantly revealing performance data which display the degree of excellence of the operational activities of the company, a single department, or a cross-functional activity.

"Each of these groups should be tracking their ten to twenty key performance indicators all the time. For example, I think this group should have, for the foreseeable future, ongoing product quality and on-time delivery as two of our key performance indicators. And soon, the engine-control project and administrative credits should be key results indicators of Bill and Elaine, respectively."

"So," said Ferg, "key results indicators are things we will track in the same way we are tracking sales growth, earnings growth, and improving return on investment now."

"Very well expressed," said Carl.

With the news he received the following week, Carl wasn't sure his voice would be deep or booming enough. The engine-control CFT had met its goal of 10 ppm.

Bill was in favor of keeping the CFT intact and driving the project to 3 ppm, but did not feel it was necessary to keep it as one of the top five. Besides, Ferg had a persuasive replacement for it.

"Let's replace it with policy, practice, and procedure hindrances," he said. "It won't be as tidy because we already have five CFTs working on it. But I feel pretty strongly that policy, practice, and procedures should be on the list."

Elaine was given the task of sponsoring this new problem and establishing what the goal would be.

Toward the end of the month, Mary Louise was able to report that Workshop 2 was completed. Ninety-seven percent of the company had attended, and the remaining 3 percent had legitimate excuses such as illness or a death in the family. They had all promised to take the workshop later.

The four-hour team leader sessions with Harvey were well attended and judged by the participants as very worthwhile.

"Are we about through with designing and installing the management stuff?" Moe asked at one of the meetings.

"Yes and no," said Carl. "It's not over, but everything is pretty much in place. From this point forward, I want this team to devote much more time to discussing the top five goals and the CFTs appointed by the mid-level CITs. We should also have more presentations from specific first-level CITs, like we had from the failure analysis team that turned in the first result and from Jason, the maintenance supervisor. We'll start this next month and shoot for spending 65 percent of our time discussing and reviewing the heart of the effort—solving operational problems and achieving operational opportunities."

At noon the next day, Ferg saw Carl in the cafeteria and suggested they take their lunches back to Carl's office. As soon as they were settled, Ferg revealed his concern.

"We haven't heard a peep about linking Continuous Improvement to P.H.C., our parent company," said Ferg. "Are you ignoring them on purpose?"

"I'm not ignoring them, but I'm not working hard on selling them on Continuous Improvement either. I've told Mr. Rumble in New York and Dr. Kristal in Amsterdam what we are doing, but they're not especially interested. If they're pleased with what we're doing, they're keeping it a secret."

"That's consistent with their past emotions, but they're busy guys," said Ferg.

"There is a potential problem on the horizon," said Carl. "The levels of defective products from our two plants are lower than what's coming out of the P.H.C. plants. Unfortunately, some of their output is going to *our* customers in the United States. They are improving—I just hope fast enough."

The next meeting signaled the first anniversary of Continuous Improvement, and Carl wanted to mark the occasion by holding an after-work session at the Fairmont Hotel for all the mid-level CIT people, followed by a buffet dinner for those who wanted to stay. Dinner was not required; attendance at the meeting was.

When Carl stepped up to the podium at 5:05 P.M., the members of the executive CIT were already sprinkled throughout the audience. In spite of appearances, this was basically an informal meeting. Carl made it clear from the beginning that he would welcome questions and observations.

"One year ago, the top staff and I first started talking about Continuous Improvement. We've come a long way since then, and I have all of you to thank for that.

"The one goal of Clear Run is to grow profitably by taking care of our customers. And what our customers want is a steady supply of new products that allow *them* to make better products at lower cost for *their* customers.

"We are applying Continuous Improvement to help meet our overall business goal of profitable growth. To do that, we are tackling five specific problems: order-to-shipment tracking; policies, practices, and procedures; the major new product; reducing defective parts shipped; and reducing customer administrative credits. All of these will help us meet our ultimate goal of profitable growth. And, if you think carefully about the three goals you have each chosen for your mid-level CITs and all the results being accomplished by the first-level CITs, it's easy to see how Continuous Improvement has already moved us toward our company goals.

"There is another side to Continuous Improvement," he said, "a very interesting side. Ninety percent of the strategic thinking about Clear Run is done by the people in this room—thinking about what products we sell to what customers and at what prices, how we are organized, how and where we manufacture products, what our people policies will be, and how well we compensate people.

"Everyone else in the company is doing the work that leads to the actual manufacturing and delivery of products to our customers. In the past we have unwittingly left them out of the thinking part—the fun part. Not because we didn't want or need their input, but because we just didn't know how to get it. But now we have a new tool: Continuous Improvement. As we use this tool, it will help make their jobs as much fun and as interesting as ours. I'm sure you've all witnessed the benefits of this. Not only is there less frustration, but hassles between groups and individuals are on the decline.

"I know a lot of you are still concerned about the two-hour-a-week guideline. Six months from now," he added, "I think we'll be able to go to a task requirement. There will be no more talk about hours per week—just the time required to do what is necessary to get the job done. But, as long as there is breath in my body, participating in Continuous Improvement will be a requirement for everyone.

"I'm not sure I need to review what we have accomplished so far. You should already be acquainted with the progress on the major goals and should have seen some of the results. From my perspective, I'm pretty pleased. I've seen many of you working together better than you ever have before. I've listened to what the first-level people have to say and have seen a sense of satisfaction in their eyes.

"Even so, there's still quite a bit of resistance, and I expect we'll keep encountering it until Continuous Improvement becomes a habit and everyone believes that we have the courage, intelligence, and persistence to make it happen.

"I want you to think of yourselves as part of a climbing expedition, led by me. Right now, we're in the middle of some very high mountains. We've just made it to our base camp at twelve thousand feet, but we have our eye on a mountain twenty thousand feet high. It's been a long, hard climb from sea level to base camp, and already certain people have decided to turn back. Doubtless, we'll lose a few more along the way. That's okay. If you don't want to see what the world looks like from the top of the mountain, that's your prerogative. But the rest of us won't rest until we've reached the summit.

"If we keep doing what we are doing—communications, appreciation, rewards, the meetings, the reviews, helping the laggards, and praising the top performers—we'll reach that next peak six months from now. Then who knows—another one, even higher, might pop into view.

"Twelve months from now, we will start incorporating Continuous Improvement into the ongoing management of the company. We'll still use the phrases *Continuous Improvement* and *cross-functional teams,* but we will no longer refer to CITs—Continuous Improvement teams. At that point, Continuous Improvement will not be a special effort. It will be the way we operate around here.

"Then we will be ready to climb even higher peaks—peaks that will represent opportunities rather than problems—opportunities to delight our customers by always being able to meet their changing requirements, by shipping products that will always meet the requirements, and by responding faster to all their needs.

"By continually setting higher and higher goals and attacking more and more problems and finding new and exciting opportunities, we'll build an internal engine that will keep driving us ahead.

"In closing, I just want to remind you that we are out of the design-and-installation part of Continuous Improvement. Clear Run could not have gotten here without you and, from the bottom of my heart, I thank you for all your help and effort. I know I can count on you, and with your persistence we will continue to improve—forever and ever. Sir Edmund Hillary has nothing on us!"

MONTH 17

■ Preparing for the eighteenth-month review

Carl woke up early on the Saturday morning of the second week of month 17. He tiptoed downstairs to his study and fired up his laptop computer to put together his thoughts for the eighteenth-month review covering the prior six months. Everything had gone reasonably well since the twelve-month mark. Sales were running 30 percent higher than they were a year ago and employment was up only 7 percent.

The screen scrolled through a list of the twenty-five CFTs and their sponsors, leaders, and problems expressed as goals. A few of them were going to have a great impact on the company—get suppliers to meet Clear Run's specifications; delight the top three customers; have a first-class preventive maintenance system; reduce accounting errors; respond to all inquiries, whether by phone, fax, or mail, by day's end; get a decent ISO 9000 certification; receive QS-9000 approval; and improve the preparation of sales calls.

He saw the goal of Elaine's new CFT there as well: remove ten major policy, practice, and procedure hindrances by month 30. That alone would help cut the time required to prepare the budget and the four-year plan and the time it took to hire new people. It would also help them improve on capital spending choices.

Carl was also pleased that Harvey, quite independently, had visited with a number of first-level CITs and persuaded them to focus on setting requirements on what was needed with their internal customers and suppliers. As a result, the computer center, for example, was starting to give better service.

He was pretty sure his top-level CIT wanted to continue meeting every week for one hour as they were convinced that this had been critical to their success so far. That was good, Carl thought, because it kept Continuous Improvement on the tip of everyone's tongue, cut down on unnecessary air time, and kept assignments in bite-size pieces.

Carl himself was finding it more and more difficult to arrange his schedule around the meetings, so Ferg, Bill, or Jim occasionally filled in for him. If Carl could attend via conference call, he did. The conference call setup seemed to be working okay, and Carol had been using it successfully with her salespeople.

It was now time to modify two items that had been put in place to force Continuous Improvement to become a habit: the two-hours-per-week guideline and the usage of first-level CITs as the only way problems could be solved by first-level people.

But before that, Carl needed to see where everything stood, so he decided to use the first three weeks of month 18 for reviews by each of the executive CIT members. Then, in the fourth week, they would agree on a course of action that would take them to month 24.

By the time the rest of the household started to stir, Carl was ready to join them for breakfast.

"I am not issuing a fixed format," Carl told his team members, who were overly concerned by the format their reports should take. "I just want you to tell us what is important. It might be your own performance rating on Continuous Improvement, the number of results forms your groups have filled out, the degree of difficulty of the problems solved and the opportunities achieved, the results of a Survey of People's Opinions, the level of people's participation, key results indicators and the performance toward their goals, how your department is using its thirty minutes per week, or how your first-level CITs are using their ten minutes a week. Tell us what have you done about resistance and poor performers. Describe your specific action committee's successes if you lead such a committee. Tell us about CFTs under your sponsorship or special surveys you've conducted. The only thing I will be firm about is hearing some of the things you plan to do over the next six months."

"How much work do you want us to put into our presentations?" asked Ferg.

"An hour or two, max," said Carl. "Everything that's important should already be in your head. Just take some time to organize your thoughts. I am not grading you on slickness here. As a matter of fact, I may subtract a few points—the flashier the presentation, the thinner the content."

"You mean Jim has to keep his Gucci shoes in the closet and his transparencies on the shelf?" asked Carol.

Jim smiled in acquiescence, but Carl could see the wheels turning in his head.

"Listen everyone," said Carl. "The three original reasons I had for doing Continuous Improvement have not changed." He held up his right index finger. "One, get results by solving operational problems and achieving operational opportunities—big ones, little ones, difficult and easy ones, the obvious and the obscure, forever and ever. Two, develop a deep concern for people. In our vision, we said we'd be firm, fair, and friendly. Now I'd like to add to that: be helpful. And three, get the basics in place so we can use some advanced techniques and methods that will propel us faster and higher.

"So, Mary Louise, Carol, and Jim, you're on for the first week of next month. Harvey, Cam, and Bill will follow the next week. And the week following that we'll hear from Moe, Ferg, and Elaine. This should lay the groundwork for the following week when we make plans for the next six months and decide what changes we need to make."

Jim didn't want the meeting to end without reminding everyone about a pending event.

"Way back when—over twelve months ago—we mentioned having an annual celebration of Continuous Improvement," said Jim. "Well, it was just a year ago that we held our first workshop and the problem-solving meetings started. So...."

"So you think it's time for another party," interrupted Carl. "Anything else you want to tell us?"

"As a matter of fact, there is. It's not really a party party. It's a fun period and a serious period combined. The communications committee is working on the plans right now. We have already engaged the vacant schoolyard right next door to us. The plan so far is to have the celebration on the last Friday of next month, starting with lunch at 1 P.M. and ending at 5 P.M."

"Anything else?"

"I'll keep you posted."

MONTH 18, WEEK 1

■ Review presentations by Mary Louise, Carol, and Jim

Mary Louise was ready to go at the first CIT meeting of the month. "I personally am very proud about the delivery and acceptance of Workshops 1 and 2 and the great results we've been getting," she said.

"When I was given this job, I understood that this method was designed to get results, do it efficiently, and embed Continuous Improvement into the fabric of the organization. The jury is still out on embedding, but I give us a 4.5 on the other two. That is better than good, but not as good as excellent.

"So far we have received ninety results forms from various teams. Some 690 people have received at least one certificate and pin. That represents just over 85 percent of our people. I would like it to be 100 percent, but I think we did pretty well for a twelve-month effort with everyone involved.

"Right now appreciation ceremonies are scheduled for every two months. So far, Carl has been present at all of them, but we might have to ease up and not expect him to make every presentation both here and in Concord.

"Continuing on results," she said, "I started building a computer database two months ago and have now entered the ninety results so that they can be sorted by person, subject, date, and department. Here is a sample," she said handing a sheet of paper to each person in the room (see p. 152), "of one of the kinds of reports you now have access to. The month, by the way, is based on the Clear Run calendar, where month 1 represents the month Carl started us all on this journey. You can also call up any of the completed results forms."

"I get good vibes from everyone on the results form," said Mary Louise. "And people tell me it's the only official writing they do that's not bound

151

Results Summary

Date*	Team	Goal	Results
6/1	Sales Unit C Casey Elsie Louise Jack Will	Improve the monthly sales forecast process within six months and improve the satisfaction index from 2.0 to 4.0 within eight months	The new process was documented within five months and the satisfaction index improved to 3.0 in seven months
6/2	Marketing Unit A Jasper Jean Susanna David Alison	Design a new way to track competitors' pricing moves on the eight months	Completed, installed, and used in six months
6/3	Legal and Sales Dept Betty Cutter Brook Margaret Bob	Within five weeks design a process so legal can comment on customers' boilerplate text on orders in less than twenty-four hours	Completed in six weeks

* Date received in Mary Louise's office.

up in some kind of a procedure. They solve the problem, write it up, send it in, and get appreciated."

"Do we have a rule on *when* in the process a team is supposed to turn in a results form?" interrupted Cam. "Do they turn it in as soon as they have solved the problem or after the goal has been attained?"

"We don't have a rule on that. The idea is to keep it simple, so as soon as the results form has the signature of the team leader's boss, it's okay.

"For the future, I want to start a collection of lessons learned. That is, as each team finds a unique solution to a problem, it fill outs a lessons learned form, which is also entered into the computer for general usage. The only problem is that it may be difficult to get people to fill them out. I'm thinking we may need some inducement, or perhaps someone could volunteer to operate like a news reporter and ferret out the lessons learned.

"I also think we should move all Continuous Improvement training into the training department and relieve the trainers from having to coach at each first-level CIT meeting. They could, however, attend if requested."

When Mary Louise was finished, Carl stood up and asked her to stand by his side.

"Mary Louise," he said, "we really appreciate you and all you've done to help launch Continuous Improvement. This," he said handing her a certificate signed by each member of the executive staff, "is a very small token of our appreciation." With that she received a very warm round of applause—and a picture of a Cadillac from Ferg.

"Sorry," he said, "but the picture is all we could get Carl to spring for."

"I'll take a cigar," she said.

Carol was next. "Well, we finally mailed out the customer survey that Ferg suggested over a year ago when we were still looking for data to justify doing Continuous Improvement. As you know, I resisted doing this survey then because I already knew we were pretty rotten as far as serving our customers. Unfortunately, the early returns aren't showing any positive surprises. The ratings are generally falling between 3.0 and 4.0, or between fair and good. The high score, 4.5, was for being pleasant and friendly. The low score, 2.0, was for ranking our ability—I should say inability—to meet the customer's needs. Comments vary, but basically they're saying, 'You're getting better, but we expect even more.'

"I feel I've personally come a long way, as has the entire sales department, since the beginning—and since Harvey helped us identify the three basic processes at work in the sales department: the process of representing our products and services to our customers and potential customers; the process of representing the customers' needs, problems, and desires back to the appropriate people at Clear Run; and the process of taking orders, changing orders, fulfilling sample requests, and dealing with defective parts, to name a few.

"My people now see that we do have problems and opportunities, and they are starting to do something about fixing them. This includes the salespeople in the field. So far we've turned in seven results forms, and three people are serving on Elaine's administrative credits CFT. Our people's opinion on Continuous Improvement is improving, and ratings from our internal customers are rising.

"Right now I'm thinking that our first key results indicator will be the amount of time we—the sales department—spend doing things that wouldn't have to be done if the people with whom we interface—our suppliers—met their requirements. After a quick little survey—face to face—I would say that the field sales force currently wastes more than 45 percent of its time and the sales support people waste more than 40 percent of their time!

"My vision for the company is 50 percent growth in sales without adding a soul to the sales department and a cessation of all hostility, bitching, whining, and complaining emanating from my department—because products will be delivered when promised, products will come without defects, questions from customers will be answered promptly, and there will be no errors in paperwork.

"I'll stop by giving us a 3.5 on actual performance, but high marks on finally grasping and starting to do something about Continuous Improvement."

"Carol," said Carl, "I'm proud of you."

Jim was next, and he was, indeed, dressed in his best suit, tie, and Gucci shoes. "Nice shoes," said Moe as Jim strode to the head of the table, donned some very dark glasses, and placed a transparency on the projector. "Go to hell. I love my Guccis and my transparencies," it said.

The initial shock was followed by a round of chuckles, and Jim removed his glasses, coat, and tie and returned to his seat.

"The marketing department is in essence following the book," he said. "I rank our performance at 4.0.

"We have no serious resistance, though we have lost five people in the last twelve months—none of them fans of Continuous Improvement—and added seven. The seven new people all signed on knowing about our Continuous Improvement effort and their required participation. I've told these new hires that we want creative, kind of wacky people, but that they need to know how to balance their wackiness with a penchant for doing things right the first time.

"As a department, marketing is physically together, so we should do a good job of listening to each other. I am not very good at listening to my people's day-to-day concerns and gripes about their own jobs. I do a much better job listening to ideas about marketing. People issues, frankly, bore me. I guess you might say that I am insensitive and impatient. I'm working on this, but it's very hard for me. If anyone has a pill I can take to cure this, I'll gladly swallow it.

"In regard to the communications specific action committee, I have been in charge for more than twelve months now. So, with the major new product right at the door, I need to start focusing on that. I suggest I be replaced as the head person on communications."

"That will be a blow to us all," said Carl.

MONTH 18, WEEK 2

- **Review presentations by Harvey, Cam, and Bill**

- **Carl speaks about his controlling style**

At the next meeting, Harvey was up first.

"The more I observe this change, the more I am convinced that progress is only made with persistence, a dogged determination to improve every day—continually, incrementally—always working for, and finding, ways to get better and better. It means running scared—believing that no matter how good you are, somewhere, someday, someone will outdo you. It means being demanding in a nonthreatening, nonpunitive way. And it requires a deep, insatiable curiosity.

"You don't need big jolts of pizzazz, or spurts of training, or reorganization, or inspirational speeches. You just need to keep doing the basics over and over and over. And that means—dare I say it once more—overcoming resistance.

"You are attending to the obvious resistance very well. But I still sense some subtle, underground resistance—the little jokes, the Dilbert cartoons, the sly digs at the effort. You still have some supervisors who slight the effort, make snide remarks, refer to the good old days, find ways to avoid problem-solving meetings, or come late and leave early. And, if they do talk about the effort, they do so without enthusiasm. You can't abide cynics. Talk to them. Let them know there's only room for people who are behind the effort 100 percent. And if you can't convince them, get rid of them.

"On a more basic level, it looks to me like first-level CITs have been doing a good job cleaning up requirements with their suppliers and customers and improving the processes within their own units. Overall, I give all of you high grades on what you are doing, how you're doing it, and the results you're getting. Keep up the good work!"

Cam was next, even anxious, with his news. "We received a surveillance audit on ISO 9000 last week and were given high praise on our new methodology...." He was interrupted by a stirring round of applause. "Wait," he said, holding up his hand. "There's more. We are also close to getting QS-9000 approval—that is, the tough quality standard established by the automotive industry for *its* suppliers. We had a bit of a head start there, because of our work on the engine-control project. Anyway, with those two under our belt and our command of Continuous Improvement, we are in a very good position to apply for the MBNQA.

"Now, if you'll look around the room," he said, pointing to the graphs permanently posted along the walls, "you'll see our key results indicators and other charts. There is one for the quality level of products shipped to each of our top seven customers and one for all of our other customers combined. There's also one for quality levels by product family, customer credits for administrative reasons, and manufacturing yield by the major processes, not to mention the charts of the top five goals and the charts of many of the CFT goals.

"As you may recall, our goal was three hundred defective parts per million shipped by month 18. I am pleased to report that we are at that level now. Many product lines are below that. However, we do have two product families at 750 and 700 ppm. Products from our sister companies average 500 ppm, and the new product will probably be shipped at somewhere between 400 and 1,000 ppm. So, we still have quite a bit of work left to reach the next level—30 ppm by month 36.

"As far as the future goes, I want to make a recommendation. We, that means all of us here today, are not comfortable with statistics—the collection and tabulation of numbers in such a way that they mean something. Knowing statistics will help us become more analytical and help reveal what is possible to attain.

"I've already talked to Jeff, our statistician, about this. He has put together an outline for a course to introduce some of the basic concepts. The material can be covered in a six-hour workshop that I think everyone in the company should be required to attend.

"Okay, so much for the good and the bad. Now for the ugly. I do have one last thing to say. Part of my job—and I am afraid it's the most visible part of my job—involves blowing the whistle to stop off-specification materials and products from traveling from one department to another or out to the customer."

"If you didn't," said Carol, "those characters of Bill's would ship the kitchen sink if they could fit it into a box."

"That's true, but it's not their fault. We define a 'good' product as one that can get by quality control. As a result, the people in production don't think about making *good* products. They think about how they'll sneak it by us, bully or threaten us into passing it, or tell a few fibs about it.

"The problem is that they are judged and paid on high volume and low cost—not on quality. So it all comes down to me. When we purchase off-spec material and it gets into a process, Bill doesn't call our purchasing agent—he calls *me* and works *me* over. When a customer complains to Carl, he doesn't call Bill, who makes the stuff—he calls me. And Carol, who do *you* call when a customer complains?"

"Who should I call?" she asked.

"How about calling the people who made it?" replied Cam. "Shouldn't they be held accountable for their own work?"

There was a long pause.

"When my department finds a product, material, process, or machine setting that is not to specifications, I should just have to tell the person or people doing the work; it should be up to *them* to decide to fix it or not to fix it. My job should simply be to audit the situation, to do the testing, and to give them the information, among other things.

"I'll still have plenty to do," said Cam. "But if I'm not always playing the role of policeman, I think I'll be much more valuable to the organization. Then I and all the quality managers in the land can send our whistles to the Smithsonian to be displayed as relics of the early days of quality control."

Cam sat down.

"Cam's right," said Ferg. "We've got to change, but we can't until everybody understands that quality is part of their job. And that comes back to us. We, as top management, need to change how the production people are measured, appreciated, and rewarded."

"Hear, hear," said Bill, whose turn was next. "As far as the rest of operations goes, I give us a 4.0. We've come a long way this past year, but we still have miles to go. So, I don't want to replace product quality on the list of our top five goals. I want to continue it with a new goal of 30 ppm by month 36. And the reason I want to do this is twofold. It's vital to meeting our customers' needs and it's one of the two best methods for measuring that all the manufacturing processes are being continually improved."

"What's the other best method?" asked Elaine.

"The other is throughput time—in other words, speed," answered Bill.

"Now, Mary Louise has arranged for some of us to visit two of the local MBNQA winners. This will let us see Continuous Improvement in action and give us some insight into what is involved in the application.

"As far as the future is concerned, I'm not too young to remember John F. Kennedy challenging the nation to land a person on the moon. What I have in mind is not nearly as ambitious, but many of you will think it is an equally outrageous goal.

"In our assembly operation, it currently takes ten days for the various pieces that make up a part to be turned into a finished part. However, we actually only *work* on the part for less than sixty minutes. The rest of the time, the pieces are waiting in front of machines. What I envision is reducing those ten days to two hours—start to finish. If we can do that, we will really get ahead of everyone else in the industry."

"Outrageous," said Jim, as Bill took his seat. "That is just the kind of thinking we need."

"In the few minutes left I want to talk a little more about the controlling management methods prevalent in the company," said Carl, "which is probably a direct result of *my* controlling ways. Once upon a time, not so very long ago, when I worked for a different company, I was promoted from marketing manager to CEO. The problem was I still really wanted to be involved in the advertising program and I had a hard time keeping my mitts off it. I finally told my replacement that I didn't want to see any copy for approval, but if I ever saw an ad I didn't think was so hot, I would give him my opinion. It worked out very well. I kept an eye on things, and he was free to do the job he was hired for. Much to my surprise, he did it very well without me. I guess I must have forgotten that lesson along the way.

"The point I want to make is that you don't have to abdicate responsibility—I did, after all, keep an eye on what he was doing—but you do have to build a way to delegate sensibly.

"This is something we all need to work on, but let's do it on an individual basis. If I'm all over any of you like a cheap suit, I hereby give you the right to tell me and we'll work it out together. Likewise, if I'm overdemanding about meeting goals to a point that nobody wants to take a risk or stick their neck out to do something great, please let me know."

MONTH 18, WEEK 3

- **Review presentations by Moe, Ferg, and Elaine**

- **Cold beans bet payoff**

The following week, Moe wasted no time before delivering the news that everyone was waiting for.

"Carl," he said, "I hope you still have that can opener—it's cold beans tonight for you and me." Everyone in the room started to cheer. "We met our goal," shouted Moe, over the uproar, "with one week to spare!"

When the room quieted down, he continued his report. "Inventory of the major new product as of today is at ten thousand pieces, and last week we issued the official press release announcing the product for sale. We also had a secondary goal for customer satisfaction, and from what we have heard from our customers so far, this should be easily met. In any case, *that* was not included in the bet.

"As for a rating, I give new products a 3.5. We met our goal and we used Continuous Improvement to get there, but we are not drenched in Continuous Improvement. I'm hoping that will change, however, as my group moves on to other products.

"With that in mind, I have been looking into some advanced Continuous Improvement techniques. One of these is called *parallel design*. That is, at the beginning of a new product design, we assemble a team of people from sales, marketing, operations, and design to work together. The idea, of course, is to speed up the whole process. At the same time, we need to pay close attention to designing products that can be manufactured inexpensively at very low defect levels to begin with, rather than having to play catch-up later.

"I think using these advanced techniques may be a good way to encourage my people in new products to build good practices into their work without plastering a big 'Continuous Improvement' label on it. It might be an easier pill for them to swallow that way. In any case, we will continue to find problems and fix them and be good suppliers and customers."

"Short but sweet," said Carl as Moe turned the floor over to Ferg.

"I am pleased with *all* the administrative departments," said Ferg. "So far we've turned in twenty-two results forms, and 90 percent of the people in administration have received a certificate and a pin. The problems solved were quite solid—very little fluff—and the thirty- and ten-minute meetings are still taking place. Results from the Survey of People's Opinions were uniformly right around 4.0 for all departments, and resistance seems to be modest. We do have some zealots—people with 'Continuous Improvement' tattooed on their foreheads who volunteer to serve on every team. We also have some soldiers who do the job with little muss, fuss, or feathers. Our internal customers recently rated us at 4.0.

"Now for the not-so-good news.

"We've hit a couple of bumps with the order-to-shipment tracking system. One was assuming that everyone using the system knew how to operate a computer. We also assumed they could type. Once the complaints started coming in, it took two months for a problem-solving team to figure out that the problem wasn't the system at all, but the operators' training. They are now trained and we are up to speed.

"The other bump had to do with pride. I suppose it was pride. When we first started the project, we had to write a lot of the software ourselves because it simply wasn't available. In the meantime, software became available for keeping track of products in our manufacturing clean rooms, but our consultants and our own software people felt *they* needed to write this software. They also thought they could do a better job. Turns out they couldn't. Finally, after a little arm twisting, we managed to convince them to purchase a clean-room tracking system.

"In spite of the bumps, I think we're still on schedule. So, Carl, I wouldn't give up your dancing lessons quite yet."

"Cold beans. Dancing for the troops. Did I make any other bets?" asked Carl, feigning concern.

"No," said Bill. "But you should have. Your losing helps the rest of us."

"Before you all get carried away," said Ferg, "you better let me finish. Once the system goes on-line, all the schedulers, including the head of operations scheduling, will be replaced by the computer. Some will be trained to do new work with the new system, and we do have spots for the others, but that top guy will be a problem."

"Why can't he be the process owner and make sure all parts of the order-to-shipment tracking system are operating as specified?" asked Elaine.

"He could, but that job classification will be lower than his current job as head of operations scheduling. Besides, the job requirements are very different. Needless to say, he's not happy about it. But we'll find something for him.

"In regard to Mary Louise's suggestion that human resources handle all Continuous Improvement training from now on, I think it's a good one. We can, if need be, beef up the training by purchasing training or sending people to special courses. We'll also work on supplying training that will help individuals fulfill their personal ambitions. This is extremely important to Carl and should be to all of us.

"And yes, it is time to formally include Continuous Improvement as part of each person's performance review. As you know, we have been promoting people and giving rewards on the basis of their on-the-job performance. Now we need to make sure that these people are also solid contributors to Continuous Improvement."

Carl interrupted. "We know that 'money' is working in at least one case," he said. "Just after we announced the Continuous Improvement bonus, one of the guys from Jim's department was walking down the hall, humming and snapping his fingers. 'I just heard that thirty of the one hundred possible bonus points for this year are for Continuous Improvement,' he told me. 'That's a language I understand.'"

Ferg rolled his eyes and shook his head. "See, this is how the world works. Knowing that, we should probably have a bonus system for everyone."

"Ferg and I have been working on that," interrupted Carl again. "We may have some news as early as next week."

"There is one more thing I want to talk about," continued Ferg, "something called *benchmarking*. What it means is that we contact some company that's doing a world-class job on something we also do. By comparing ourselves to that company, we should be able to see many ways in which we can improve. I want to do this with one or two of my departments in the future."

As Elaine took over the meeting, the expression on Carl's face turned from pleased to smug. He knew he had saved the best for last.

"We give ourselves a 4.0 on the number of results forms we turned in and on the participation," said Elaine. "I have found it very effective to ask people in the department, 'If we were a separate finance and accounting firm, would Clear Run be willing to hire us?' The answer is supposed to be yes. Just to make sure, we continually measure our customers' satisfaction. In a recent poll with about thirty key users, the average was 4.2, which isn't bad, but we did have a few 3.0s. Our goal as of now is 4.5 with nothing under 4.0. We still have a ways to go in that area—but not in customer administrative credits.

"As you know, I have sponsored that CFT, and our original goal was to have only 0.3 percent credits by month 18. Well, with a lot of help from Carol's department, the product engineers, and shipping, we have been under 0.3 percent for the last two months. I have already assigned one of the accounting people to be the process owner and thus permanently accountable to see that this key results indicator keeps improving. Therefore, I think we should remove this goal from our list of the top five.

"We really haven't discussed savings, as such, but I thought I'd show you what we've done anyway. One of our people spent eight hours reviewing the results forms and then talked to a few of the team leaders, who indicated they'd had some big savings. We calculated that we have saved $3.7 million in direct costs over the last twelve months as a direct result of Continuous Improvement."

Elaine was briefly interrupted by a stirring round of applause before raising her hand for quiet. "I did a few more hours' work and calculated that the capital spending to obtain these savings was about $625,000. I'll let you do the rest of the math."

"Does that drop right into net profits?" asked Moe, incredulously.

"Yes, but it becomes mingled with the effects of other things. For example, some of these savings are eaten away by price declines because we matched our competitors' pricing or because we lowered our prices to expand our market. And, of course, the costs of what we purchase are always increasing. So, if we didn't have these savings as a contributor, our bottom line would probably be suffering right about now."

"Do you have a simple way for a team to calculate its own savings and add it to its results form?" asked Bill.

"Funny you should ask," said Elaine, picking up a stack of paper and passing it around the room. "I just happen to have a very simple way to do it (see p. 163). Once you've figured out how to calculate the savings, follow the example to display those savings and benefits in a format we can all use, just to keep everything uniform.

"And, by the way," Elaine added, "to keep Continuous Improvement on the straight and narrow, projected annual savings should only be counted once. If, in subsequent years, there are additional savings, those savings may be counted.

A Way to Calculate Savings

An easy way for everyone in the organization to calculate savings is to calculate annual direct or out-of-pocket savings. Direct savings can come only from not having to pay someone or not having to purchase something.

1. Estimate the number of person-hours not used if the change were made.
2. Calculate how many hours that represents over one year.
3. Multiply that by the person's hourly pay, including other monetary benefits.
4. Determine savings, on an annual basis, of material not used.
5. Add the two calculations together.

Example
1. The estimated savings from the new proofreading process is 3 hours and 30 minutes per week.
2. 48 weeks × 3.5 hours per week = 168 hours per year.
3. For a person who earns $20 an hour, $20 per hour × 168 hours = $3,360 per year saved.
4. $8,000 saved through material not wasted.
5. $3,360 + $8,000 = $11,360 projected annual savings.

Examples of Projected Annual Savings and Benefits

Date	Item	Projected Annual Savings	Who Benefits
3/1	Improved mailing list	$17,000	Marketing
3/2	New preventive maintenance method	$62,000	Operations
3/4	New proofreading process	$11,360	Marketing

"The new top-five goal—remove ten major policy, practice, or procedure hindrances by month 30—is well under way. We've already knocked off three, and three more have been assigned to CFTs.

"That's it, except for one last thing. Let's add one outrageous goal to our top five and shift into high gear!"

"Thanks Elaine, for your presentation and your thoughts on a new goal," said Carl. "We'll talk more about that next week, assuming I survive tonight's dinner."

Carl and Moe arrived at the Chicken Box at 5:30 P.M. on the nose, where a large sign was already hanging over the door.

Winning Engineers—Hot BBQ
Moe & Carl—Cold Beans

A reporter and photographer for *Clear Run to Number One* were waiting by the curb. Moe and Carl obliged them by posing under the sign with their arms thrown over each other's shoulders, giving a big thumbs up. As they walked through the door, someone passed Moe and Carl cold water in tin cups—their beverage for the evening. Just about everyone else was brandishing an ice cold beer.

The Chicken Box was a favorite haunt of the engineers, and they had reserved it until 8:30 that night. They had also invited their wives, husbands, girlfriends, and boyfriends. Anticipating the celebratory nature, a two-beer limit had been imposed, but recognizing that it would be virtually impossible to enforce, Darryl had a couple of vans available to take people home.

Once dinner was ready, Moe and Carl were led to the table of dishonor. Six of the engineers ceremoniously emerged from the kitchen with two hot barbecue dinners and two cans of beans. Calling for silence, the leader of the procession shouted, "All in favor of hot barbecue for Carl and Moe, say aye." There were a few ayes, which were barely audible over the boos and jeers from the rest of the crowd. "All opposed, say nay." The enthusiasm was deafening. Thumbs pointed down, and the two plates of barbecue were ceremoniously carried away.

Carl whipped out his can opener and was at his beans in a flash. Moe, who had never used anything but an electric can opener his entire life, went hungry until Carl mercifully opened his can for him.

The engineers were flying. As the barbecue dinners were devoured, hats appeared. Over the visor they read, "Let them eat beans." One after another, the three engineering supervisors rose and simply thanked everyone present for their terrific effort and accomplishment. The last one ended by thanking Moe and Carl for their foolish judgment. "Let this be a lesson to you," she said. "Never bet against the engineers!"

MONTH 18, WEEK 4

- ■ **Actions on issues from the review presentations**
- ■ **Plans for the next six months**

Carl had a week to recover before it was his turn to address the weekly meeting of the executive CIT.

"I want to thank all of you for bringing us up to speed over the last three weeks. Your progress, on all counts, is truly commendable. I particularly appreciate your comments regarding items that need immediate attention. To wit," he said, producing a large sheet of chart paper, "I have prepared this little list."

He read off each item on the list. "Move Continuous Improvement training to the human resources training department. Require attendance at a six-hour statistics workshop. Stop requiring trainers to coach at every first-level CIT problem-solving meeting. Pay more attention to listening. Replace Jim as head of the communications specific action committee. Change or remove the Continuous Improvement cynics. Decide to keep or replace the product quality goal as a top-five goal. Select two new problems with goals to replace the major new product and the customer administrative credits on the list of the top five. Include Continuous Improvement in personal performance reviews. Make sure people who receive financial and nonfinancial rewards have contributed positively to Continuous Improvement. Consider applying for MBNQA. Allow first-level CIT problem-solving teams to move to the CFT format. Remove the two-hours-per-week-per-person guideline.

"With the exception of the last two items, which I added, each item on this list was something you mentioned in your reviews," said Carl.

"Since no one complained about the percentage of time being spent on Continuous Improvement, I assumed it is not an issue and that I'm not pushing you into a lot of work that you feel is unnecessary.

"I was also especially pleased to hear about some of your plans for the future. Bill's outrageous goal on throughput time, Mary Louise's plans to collect lessons learned, Moe's on focusing on parallel engineering and better designing, Ferg's on training of individuals and benchmarking, Elaine's on being the finance and accounting department of choice and presenting savings data, Jim's on going after the next round of new products, Carol's observation on how to make a more effective sales department, and, Cam, the elimination of your role as policeman.

"What I'd like to do now is to discuss what we can do about each item on this list."

For the next hour they tackled them one by one and, without much ado, reached the following agreements: move Continuous Improvement training to the human resources training department; have Jeff design and pilot a course in statistics that, if successful, would be required of everyone in the organization; have trainers' coaching at problem-solving meetings be by invitation only; have Mary Louise replace Jim as head of the communications specific action committee; find and root out the cynics; and include Continuous Improvement in personal performance reviews, along with promoting and rewarding only those who are solid performers in Continuous Improvement.

Listening was put on the agenda for a future meeting because it seemed such an individual thing. Cam was asked to gather the MBNQA particulars with an eye toward applying for the award, if for no other purpose than to benchmark Clear Run versus the "big boys." They also decided to postpone a discussion of financial and nonfinancial rewards for another two months to give Ferg an opportunity to hold a few committee meetings first.

"Do me a favor," added Carl, "Set a good, sensible Continuous Improvement goal with each of the top fifty people—one that their performance can be logically measured against. I don't want anybody coming to me at bonus time sniveling and crying that they were treated unfairly."

Everyone agreed to the first item Carl had added to the list—to allow first-level CFTs to be formed. This allowed supervisors the choice of having individuals solve problems in their organizational units or on special CFTs. But no one thought Continuous Improvement was far enough along to remove the guideline of two hours per week per person.

"However," Carl warned them, "we've got to remove this requirement by month 24 if we expect to fold Continuous Improvement into the ongoing management of the company.

"As you are well aware from the conversations in our regular staff meetings, I have been talking to my bosses about a yearly bonus for everyone. They have agreed to a bonus pool—with money going to each and every employee—of 10 percent of what we actually earn above our annual budgeted earnings. In a good year, this will be a bonus to each person equal to about two weeks' salary. Ferg and I will work out the details and discuss them with you."

"That's good news, very good news," said Bill. "Now everyone, to a lesser degree, will be treated like the top fifty. People will begin to see a direct relationship between their bonuses and how the company performs on Continuous Improvement."

"That's our intention," said Carl.

"I just had a thought," said Jim. "When we first started talking about Continuous Improvement, one of our big problems was people's frustration. Morale was low, people were not being used effectively, and there was poor communication. Have we made any progress on these fronts in the last eighteen months?"

"Well, our focus has been on fixing problems," said Ferg. "And lo and behold, when problems get fixed, communications improve and frustration lessens. I'd say people have started using their brains to plan, redesign, and track the performance of their own work—which makes them happier. So I'd also say that morale is definitely higher."

"Ferg," said Jim, "is there any reason we can't add a question on level of frustration to the Survey of People's Opinions and one on their level of satisfaction as well?"

"I don't see why not," said Ferg. "I'll attend to that. Now as far as communications goes, we are doing a much better job of listening even though we have a ways to go."

"Sorry, Ferg," said Jim. "Let's add something on listening to the opinion survey and to the customer survey."

"Okay," said Ferg. "Any other suggestions?"

As there were none, Carl spoke up. "As long as we're talking about people," he said, "I have a few thoughts of my own.

"We absolutely cannot have everyone cut from the same mold. True, we do need people who can and will be part of a team, but we need some geniuses as well—some very creative, very insightful people. And the place we need them most is in the creation and manufacturing of new products.

"Unfortunately, you can't go to central casting and order up one or two geniuses. However, and I'm speaking from experience, one or two never fail to appear at the most unexpected times and under the most unlikely circumstances. What we have to do is create an environment that will make these people appear, feel fulfilled, contribute to the fullest, and stay with us.

"Having said that, let me add that everyone should be treated the same way I've been treated over the years. To repeat what I said about a year ago, I have been helped when I needed it and left alone when I didn't. I have been given the right to be different, encouraged to become as good as I want to be—with full access to education—and I have been compensated justly."

"You want that for everybody? Every single person?" asked Moe.

"Why not?"

"Won't we just be investing in people who might eventually leave us?"

"I suppose so, but so what? Someone new and even better may come along, drawn to us because of who we are. Anyway, that is my vision. The question for all of us is how we make that vision a reality."

Carl then asked Ferg to lead the discussion on selecting two new top-priority goals to replace the major new product and customer administrative credits, and on deciding whether to continue with the product quality goal. Almost immediately everyone agreed to continue that one.

While everyone broke for coffee, Ferg wrote the three remaining goals on a sheet of chart paper. After the others returned, Ferg asked for suggestions on the two openings. Jim and Carol were very keen on adding "Receive no less than a 4.5 overall satisfaction index rating from each of our top ten customers by month 30."

"This would be a great indication of our customers' satisfaction," said Carol, "and great for us internally because we have to do so many things well to earn a 4.5. It will also be a challenge because, as I said last week, our across-the-board customer satisfaction is now 3.5."

Seeing that some were not convinced, Jim added, "Look, the engine-control part served as a flagship to improve quality on all products. A goal involving the satisfaction of our top ten customers will do the same for delighting all customers. Carol and I could sponsor a CFT to determine what specific things, other than delivery and quality, are annoying our customers. Once we know that, we can form additional CFTs to make the improvements they want."

His reasoning was persuasive enough for Ferg to add the goal to the list.

With room for just one more, Ferg decided to speak up about an idea he'd had for some time. "I've been trying to find a way to measure our concern for individuals and turn it into a goal. I think we can do it with the turnover index—the number of people who leave Clear Run in any year for any reason, divided by our total head count. We wouldn't include people who died, decided to attend college full time, or who had to accompany a spouse who was moving. That would leave us with a number for people who leave each year because we can't or won't give them a job that excites them.

"If we could reduce the turnover rate by 50 percent over the next eighteen months, that would be a pretty good indication that we were showing progress in this area."

Carl was particularly pleased with this one, and after a short discussion Ferg added it to the list.

"I'll be the sponsor on this one," he said, "but really, all the work to make it happen rests with each of you."

By the end of the meeting, the new top five goals were in place.

Top Five Goals

Opportunity	Goal	Sponsor	Team
Order-to-shipment tracking system	Less than 5 percent missed shipments to the promised dates by month 23	Ferg	CFT
Remove policy, practice, and hindrances	Ten significant improvements by month 30	Elaine	CFTs
Reduce defective parts shipped	Less than 30 ppm by month 36	Cam	Mid-level CIT
Increase satisfaction of the top ten customers	4.5 or better satisfaction index rating from each customer by month 30	Jim	CFTs
Reduce adjusted turnover rate	Fifty percent reduction by month 36	Ferg	Mid-level CIT

"Which ones are outrageous?" asked Elaine. "Are we are really stretch-ing here?"

"The two new ones have plenty of stretch in them," said Carl. "If we hit both of them, we'll know we're really special. And I assume Bill will be working on his manufacturing-time reduction goal and Moe will start to get new products to market much, much faster with parallel engineer-ing. So we have two outrageous goals on the horizon."

The following afternoon was set aside so the entire company could celebrate Clear Run's first Continuous Improvement anniversary. It had been a little over a year since the kickoff meeting, and everyone in the company had become involved. At noon, they all hustled over to the school next door, where the sun shone brightly on a tent positioned in the middle of the soccer field. A huge banner greeted everyone as they arrived: "Clear Run—Celebration Day—Continuous Improvement." A band from the local high school was playing ragtime music as people picked up their drinks and box lunches.

Members of each of the major departments could be identified by their different colored T-shirts with their own celebration-day logo silk-screened on the front.

At 1:30 a whistle blew, and everyone wandered into the tent and took a seat. A stage was set up in front, with seats for Carl and Ferg and two other people no one else recognized. One was the director of purchasing for the automotive company that purchases the engine-control part and the other was the president of one of Clear Run's suppliers.

Each took a turn addressing the crowd. Ferg thanked everyone for a job well done and mentioned a few teams and a few people who had done some really special Continuous Improvement work. Each of the two guests spoke about the benefits that Clear Run's Continuous Improvement effort had bestowed upon them. Carl closed with a summary of the eighteenth-month review and displayed the new list of the top five Con-tinuous Improvement goals.

At 2:30 everyone headed back outside for relay races, a wheelbarrow race, an egg and spoon race, an egg toss, a football throw for distance and another for accuracy, and a relay race involving bobbing for apples. The grand finale was a tug-of-war between departments. Carol's team from sales handily defeated Moe's team from new products.

At 4:00 they all returned to the tent, picking up ice cream cones and soft drinks along the way.

Ferg announced the gold, silver, and bronze winners for each event, amid cheers and boos. Then everyone was entertained by skits spoofing Continuous Improvement that were presented by members of each of the six major departments.

The last and biggest laugh-getter was a production team of seven strangely costumed people sitting around a table staring at a chart stand covered with gibberish. "But that is not good enough!" one of them yelled. "Not good enough at all! We must make the *right* error the first time!"

At 5:00 the winners of the games picked up their trophies, and everyone headed home.

MONTH 24

■ Transitioning Continuous Improvement into the fabric of Clear Run

As Carl drove to the office, he checked the date on the newspaper beside him and thought, "This is the exact day, two years ago, that we had our very first meeting on Continuous Improvement. Boy, what a change. And today we start another change—folding Continuous Improvement into the fabric of the company and running it with all the other things we do."

The effort had gone well over the last six months, and practically all the signs were positive. There was still some resistance here and there, but in the interim another eighty results forms had been turned in, spread pretty evenly throughout the company. Of these, twenty-three were CFTs that had met their goals or met significant milestones toward their goals. That made a total of 170 teams that had been formally appreciated over the last eighteen months. Mary Louise was now plant manager of the Sudbury plant, and Cam had agreed to take over her role as the CI counselor on a part-time basis. He could do this because he was no longer playing the role of policeman.

Quarterly sales were running 35 percent higher than a year ago, but employment was only up 11 percent. Continuous Improvement couldn't claim all the credit for that because a lot of labor-saving equipment had been installed. But even so, the number of people outside the plants had increased only 15 percent. Earnings were glorious, and they had handled this business surge with less hassle, less frustration, and fewer unhappy customers than they had during any of the prior booms.

"Yes," thought Carl as he pulled into his parking slot, "things are going pretty well."

Carl opened the meeting with a few classic lines of verse:

"'The time has come,' the Walrus said,

'To talk of many things:

Of shoes—and ships—and sealing-wax—

Of cabbages—and kings—'"

There were a few puzzled looks, but others in the room recognized the lines from Lewis Carroll's *Through the Looking Glass* and smiled broadly.

"When we first started discussing this effort two years ago," Carl began, "we used special names such as CITs, CFTs, CI counselor, and specific action committees. We've now reached a point where we no longer want Continuous Improvement to be different and separate; we want *one* management method and *one* culture. This does not mean that Continuous Improvement will receive one iota less attention or produce one jot fewer improvements. It just means it will no longer stand alone as a separate entity.

"Strategic goals and financial budget goals have always gathered the major attention of management and should continue to receive major attention. Continuous Improvement goals are to be added to those two— and to be of equal importance.

"So, I would like to drop the terms *top-level CIT, mid-level CIT,* and *first-level CIT,* along with the guideline of meeting one hour, thirty minutes, and ten minutes per week. Instead, all levels of management should meet as often and as long as they see fit to meet their Continuous Improvement goals. Unit meetings to solve a particular problem can still be called first-level CITs or CFTs, whichever is more appropriate. But the phrase *specific action committee* should disappear from our lexicon."

"Hold everything!" said Bill. "Are you saying that we won't be meeting an hour a week on Continuous Improvement?"

"No," said Carl, "what I'm saying is that we can meet as often as we wish and invite whomever we want to our meeting to deal with Continuous Improvement matters."

"Even so," said Moe, "I think we should still take the first hour of our three-hour weekly staff meeting for Continuous Improvement."

"That's fine," agreed Carl. "As long as we stop calling ourselves the 'executive CIT.'

"We'll keep the four principles of Continuous Improvement and incorporate them into the list of beliefs and principles in our employee brochures. Our vision statement will be part of our four-year plan, which, by the way, will be available to everyone in the company in a four- to six-page summary. Communication on Continuous Improvement will be threaded into our existing internal and external communications."

"Wait a minute," protested Carol. "I put my foot down on killing *Clear Run to Number One*."

Everyone, Jim in particular, laughed, remembering Carol's reluctance during the first few weeks of the effort.

"We can continue to publish *Clear Run to Number One* for another year," said Jim. "Then we can think about combining it with our regular newsletter."

Carl continued, "Continuous Improvement training has already been moved to the human resources department, and we will merge Continuous Improvement appreciation and rewards with our other ongoing methods of recognition, using the best of each to create one system that covers everything.

"My last comments concern the very heart of Continuous Improvement," he said, "the finding of problems and opportunities, the setting of goals, and being accountable for results. I think this should all be moved into our existing financial budgeting and management-by-objective systems, which are already institutionalized. This way, I think we can guarantee that Continuous Improvement will continue to deliver results with the same passion and persistence that it has over the last eighteen months.

"Given all that, it should take us about two or three months to move Continuous Improvement into the ongoing management of the company. We'll then have one Clear Run culture and one way to do things—the right way."

"Whoa, Carl. That's pretty glib," said Bill. "Just do this. Just do that. We've just finally become comfortable with this method, and now you want to change everything."

"Well," said Carl, "I told you way back when that my ultimate goal was to weave Continuous Improvement into the fabric of the organization or its impact would be pretty short term. Mark my words, there will be no less effort by anyone and no less expectation from us for improvement. It's just not going to stand alone any longer. It will simply be the way we do things around here."

During the last week of the month, Carl had a full company meeting at the local theater to announce the change. The one-and-a-half-hour meeting was unaccompanied by bands and posters, but the *Clear Run to Number One* reporters and photographers were on hand.

Carl and the full top staff sat up front. Carl tapped on the mike to quiet the audience and started by reviewing the past eighteen months of Continuous Improvement's highs and lows. He announced a bonus system for all people. Then he described the process of moving Continuous Improvement into the fabric of the company, pausing for questions that either he or a member of his staff answered.

After a five-minute recess so everyone could stand up and stretch their legs, Carl tapped the mike again.

"Over the last twenty-four months, I have mentioned repeatedly my three personal reasons for doing Continuous Improvement. In case you've forgotten, I'll repeat them once more. The first is the most obvious: to solve operational problems and achieve operational opportunities. That includes big ones, little ones, the obvious, the obscure, the easy, and the difficult. The second reason is to turn on the sunshine around here—to let people's self-assurance or self-esteem flourish, to make your work more fulfilling, and to help each of you go as far as your abilities and desires can take you. The last reason is simply to learn the fundamentals of Continuous Improvement so we can move on to a whole array of advanced management techniques that will help us reach goals that will, forever, be higher and more difficult.

"These are still my top three reasons, and I continue to marvel that these three things will be accomplished by each of us continuously improving the processes of the work we do.

"In the future we'll be spending more time on operational *opportunities* because most of the problems will soon be solved. We will move from merely satisfying our customers to delighting them. And we will certainly focus on doing things faster. No goal is too outrageous. And no way to reach an outrageous goal will be beyond our grasp.

"We do have a hierarchical management system, which means for the most part that information and control come from the top down. But our work moves horizontally. So to optimize our work flows, we will need to do more horizontal managing. Continuous Improvement is a step in that direction.

"Right now, there is bold talk in the land about 'learning organizations,' and I think we are starting to be one. We will be doing more training in the future, but doing it carefully. I don't want to load the ship with a lot of courses and sail off into the sunset. We will purchase training as needed.

"The last thing I want to talk about is you and how Clear Run has and can continue to help you as an individual.

"Just asking you to help do your own work better has exercised some new brain cells, and this makes your work more interesting. You no longer just do what you are told. You first have to figure out what your customer wants, and then you have to figure out how to do it.

"I'm also happy to say that the low morale—due to frustrations, hassles, poor communication, and poor teamwork—that used to appear so consistently in the early surveys has declined sharply. This is because, by working together, we were able to find the underlying causes and fix them. Now we have a new goal: to make ten major changes to policies, practices, and procedures within six months. This should make everyone happy by cutting the amount of red tape that may currently be binding you. The net result, I hope, is that each of us will be given ample space to do our jobs to the best of our potential.

"To put our money where our mouth is, so to speak, we've added another goal: to reduce the turnover of people by 50 percent. To do that, we have to make your work more fulfilling, and that we fully intend to do. Listening to you is one thing we are trying to do better, and I hope all of you are listening as well.

"I also want all of you first-line people, supervisors and managers, to add a line to your performance review forms that tells us what you want to do in the future. For example, you might want a higher grade job, a different kind of work, or to learn to do some part of your current job better. If that's what you want, you need to let us know. Then your supervisor or manager will be responsible for helping you get the training you need, formal or informal, to learn how to do that work. And the training department will focus on providing that kind of training.

"I believe that if we do these things, our turnover will fall by 50 percent and any survey will show that a very high percentage of people are fully satisfied with their career paths at Clear Run.

"I've said it before, and I'll say it again: in two to three years most of us will run—not walk—to work because it's a pleasure to deal with our peers and because we have all helped ourselves improve."

Epilogue

Twenty-three months from the day Carl first summoned his executive staff to his office to start discussions on Continuous Improvement, the order-to-shipment tracking system met its goal of less than 5 percent missed shipments to promised date. This performance was maintained for sixteen consecutive weeks. True to his word, Carl paid off yet another bet at the Clear Run Christmas party.

"Carl," said Ferg, stopping the music for a moment, "it's midnight, and you're not turning into a pumpkin until you perform."

The orchestra struck up "Sweet Georgia Brown" as Carl grabbed the microphone and proceeded to sing in a strong, clear voice while dancing a snappy two-step. Then, after picking his wife out of the crowd that circled the floor, they danced as one before gliding back to the mike, where Carl coaxed everyone into singing a reprise of the first verse as he bowed and waved to them all.

One year later, Carl retired. Shortly thereafter, someone overheard Carl's successor comment on Continuous Improvement and Clear Run.

"Embedded?" he had said. "I couldn't blast Continuous Improvement out of this company if my life depended upon it!"

APPENDIX I

The Fifteen Parts
of Continuous Improvement

The fifteen parts are presented here as a number of suggested actions with references to pages where they are applied in the story.

1. **Understand the Method and Organizational Structure**
   ■ Select a method of Continuous Improvement, 7–18
   PLUS
   > Continuous Improvement, definition of, 1
   > history, 1–2
   > change process, definition of, 2, 43
   > timeline, 22–23, 82
   > treat people to get the best out of them, 29, 81–82, 144, 160, 168
   > learn by starting, 39
   > decision to proceed, 39–40, 52, 56–57, 64, 67–68
   > culture change, definition of, 43
   > alternative ways, 55–56
   > Carl's reasons for proceeding, 57, 78, 149, 176
   > solve problems now, 74, 84
   ■ Form CITs, CFTs, and specific action committees and establish their duties and meeting habits, 7–18
   PLUS
   > vertical (hierarchical) vs. horizontal organization, 27–28, 176
   > specific action committees, 30, 40, 73
   > weekly meetings, 30, 36, 68, 85
   > top-level CIT guidelines, 42–43
   > first-level CIT guidelines, 84, 88, 91, 93, 99–101, 105, 147, 156
   > meeting space, 85, 96
   > CFT guideline, 93

13. Appreciate and Reward Achievement

■ Appreciate people, 114–115, 117
  PLUS
      Jim, Bill, Ferg, Carol, and Cam appreciated, 56
      Carl appreciated, 112
      ANs (appreciation notes), 132
      appreciation ceremony, 136–137, 151
      thin vs. thick results, 141
      cigar as appreciation, 141
      Mary Louise appreciated, 153
      Carol appreciated, 154
■ Reward people, 115–116
  PLUS
      promoted and rewarded people—must be solid contributors to Continuous Improvement, 161
      bonuses, 161, 166–167, 176

14. Modify Prior Operating Guidelines

■ Modify prior operating guidelines, 165–169
  PLUS
      personal performance reviews, 104, 161, 177
      top-level CIT's new allocation of tasks, 143
      two-hour-per-week-per-person guideline, 144, 148, 174
      first-level CITs may move to the CFT format, 148
      lessons learned, 152–153
      coaches no longer required, 153
      new CI counselor, part time, month 24, 173

15. Transition Continuous Improvement into the Ongoing Management of the Organization

■ Transition Continuous Improvement into the ongoing management, 173–177
■ Use advanced techniques
      ISO 9000, 3, 137, 156
      experts, 65, 124, 136
      treat people to get the best out of them, 81–82, 144, 160, 168, 176–177
      statistics, 121, 156, 166
      QS-9000, MBNQA, 137–138, 156, 158, 166
      parallel design, 159
      process owner, 161–162
      benchmarking, 161
      learning organization, 176

APPENDIX II

Designing, Installing, and Operating a Continuous Improvement Effort

Organizations with twenty-five to two thousand people, and two to five layers of management, should stay close to the story's timetable and organizational structure.

Organizations with fewer than twenty-five people could move faster during the first twelve weeks and apply the fifteen parts in any way they see fit.

Organizations with more than two thousand people could use the method by applying it to sections of the organization, with no more than two thousand people per section and no more than five layers of management. The very top person in the organization must establish the roles and responsibilities for himself or herself and the superstructure of managers between the top layer and the heads of the individual sections. He or she might want to seek advice on how to do this from an expert in organization behavior.

Organizations already doing Continuous Improvement should start at the beginning of the story, continuing with those things already in place and eliminating those things they are doing that are not helpful.

All fifteen parts must be used to meet the three purposes of the design: get plenty of results, get them efficiently, and get Continuous Improvement embedded in the fabric of the organization. How the fifteen parts are used should be a sensible blend between what fits your organization and what worked for Clear Run.

The importance of each activity is made clear by the amount of time spent on it and the frequency and passion with which it is mentioned. For example, the results form is referred to time and again. It is critical.

However, lessons learned is mentioned only once; it is necessary for but not critical to success.

The timetable presented in the story is merely an indicator of what can be accomplished in twenty-four months. Some organizations might move more quickly and others more slowly. Once the problem-solving training starts, keep the pressure on, erring if need be on the side of moving too fast. Deliberation and sluggishness are deadly—there are too many other forces at play that could push Continuous Improvement off the high burners.

APPENDIX III

Discussion Groups

Group discussions have proven to help develop a deep, universal understanding of Continuous Improvement among people whose knowledge, experience, and opinions may be quite diverse. To launch a successful Continuous Improvement effort, such discussion groups could be initiated by the top-level CIT and led by the top person in the organization. Discussion can then continue down into the organization, with each mid-level CIT doing the same.

Discussion groups should not ensue until after each person in the group has studied this book. The following list of discussion topics can serve as a guideline. Assigning each member a few topics on which he or she is to be especially prepared will help get everyone involved.

- Discuss the definition of Continuous Improvement, what complacency refers to, and the power of Continuous Improvement.
- Did Carl's executive CIT have good ways to find and select problems and opportunities? Were the problems and opportunities they selected impact issues? Would these issues help them meet their four-year plan?
- What are the fifteen parts of the change process, and how did Carl use them? Why were parts fourteen and fifteen included?
- Give some examples of resistance and how each example was reduced, worn down, or worked around.
- Discuss the various ways communications were employed to further the goals of Carl's Continuous Improvement method.
- Carl's team came up with several ways to hold people accountable. Discuss how this is an example of achieving a Continuous Improvement opportunity.

- Why is so much emphasis put on measuring improvement? In what ways is this similar to other ways of measuring performance (e.g., dollars and units) that are used in organizations?
- Discuss the various aspects of Carl's leadership capabilities, citing specific examples. Was Carl a charismatic leader or a leader with persistence? Did any of the members of his team display leadership characteristics?
- Once the effort was under way, why did Carl want to spend 65 percent of the executive CIT's time on getting problems solved and opportunities achieved?
- How were the people at Clear Run challenged and led to do better? Do you think Continuous Improvement will help make Clear Run a more entrepreneurial company—one that can change and grow in a changing world?
- To what extent did the benefits gained by Clear Run exceed the time and dollars spent?
- What were some of the advanced methods and techniques used to solve problems and achieve opportunities during the first two years? What advanced methods might be used to help solve some of the new goals Carl's team put forward in month 24?
- What was done or planned to help meet Carl's second reason for doing Continuous Improvement—"to turn on the sunshine around here, to make people's self-assurance flourish, to make their work more fulfilling, and to help them go as far as their abilities and desires can take them"?
- In what ways could Carl and his executive CIT have modified their approach and still met their expectations to solve many problems and achieve many opportunities, to complete the effort quickly and efficiently, and to end up with Continuous Improvement embedded in the organization?

APPENDIX IV

Where to Find Out More About
ISO 9000, QS-9000, and the MBNQA

For further information about ISO 9000, contact:
The American Society for Quality
611 East Wisconsin Avenue
P.O. Box 3005
Milwaukee, WI 53201-3005
Phone: 414-272-8578
Fax: 414-272-1734

For further information about QS-9000, call:
Automotive Industry Action Group
Phone: 810-358-3003

The application for the Malcolm Baldrige National Quality Award is first
filled out by the organization and then reviewed by MBNQA examiners,
who review the approach, deployment, and results of an organization's
leadership, strategic planning, customer and market focus, information
and analysis, human resource development and management, process
management, and business results. For further information, contact MBNQA,
and ask for Criteria for Performance Excellence, Application Forms, and
Instructions:
Malcolm Baldrige National Quality Award
Phone: 301-975-2036
Fax: 301-948-3716

Or contact:

The American Society for Quality
Phone: 414-272-8578
Fax: 414-272-1734

Index